# Reach You[...]

# ARIES

Teresa Moorey

# Dedication

To Jonathan, my son and 'special Aries',
and to Annie, my sister,
and to Ken Moorey

Orders: please contact Bookpoint Ltd, 39 Milton Park, Abingdon, Ozon OX14 4TD. Telephone: (44) 01235 400414, Fax: (44) 01235 400454. Lines are open from 9.00–6.00, Monday to Saturday, with a 24 hour message answering service. Email address: orders@bookpoint.co.uk

*British Library Cataloguing in Publication Data*
A catalogue record for this title is available from The British Library

ISBN 0 340 69709 1

First published 1998
Impression number  11   10   9   8   7   6   5   4   3   2
Year                          2004      2003      2002      2001      2000      1999      1998

Typeset by Transet Limited, Coventry, England.
Printed in Great Britain for Hodder & Stoughton Educational, a division of Hodder Headline plc, 338 Euston Road, London NW1 3BH by Cox and Wyman, Reading, Berks.

# Contents

# Introduction

## A PERSPECTIVE OF ASTROLOGY

Interest in the mystery and significance of the heavens is perhaps as old as humankind. If we can cast our imaginations back, to a time when there were no street lamps, televisions or even books, if we can picture how it must have been to have nothing to do through the deep nights of winter other than to sit and weave stories by the fire at the mouth of our cave, then we can come close to sensing how important the great dome of stars must have seemed in ancient times.

We are prone to believe that we are wiser today, having progressed beyond old superstitions. We know that all stars are like our Sun – giant nuclear reactors. We know that the planets are lumps of rock reflecting sunlight, they are not gods or demons. But how wise are we in truth? Our growing accumulation of facts brings us no closer to discovering the real meaning behind life – in fact the mountain of science can sometimes bar the way to the only path that really matters. This is the path of questions that are more important than answers – the path that offers occasional tantalising glimpses of panoramas beyond our usual ordinary vision. It could also be called the path that seeks the holistic vision, where we can perceive ourselves as part of a meaningful cosmos. It may well be that our cave-dwelling ancestors knew better than us the meaning of holism. The study of astrology may be part of a journey towards a more holistic perception, taking us, as it does, through the fertile, and often uncharted realms of our own personality.

## ■ THE HISTORY OF ASTROLOGY

Until the seventeenth century astrology (which searches for the meaning of heavenly patterns) and astronomy (which seeks to clarify facts about the skies) were one, and it was the search for meanings, not facts that inspired the earliest investigations. Lunar phases have been found carved on bone and stone figures from as early as 15,000BCE (Before Common Era). Astronomical observations were important in timing migrations, floods and seasonal changes for the Stone Age hunter-gatherer tribes, and this became even more essential as agriculture developed. However, the motions of the heavens were also regarded as a metaphor for human life, from birth to death. Spiritual motives no doubt empowered the construction of megalithic complexes such as Stonehenge, Avebury and Carnac, which are built to reflect the movements of Sun and Moon. The knowledge of these cultures may have been communicated to Mesopotamia, where astrology as we know it was formed and incubated from a combination of astronomy and mythology.

Astrological techniques began to be developed around 2000BCE, but 'modern' astrology was born only when Greek culture combined with Mesopotamian skills at the time of the conquests of Alexander the Great, around 300BCE. The earliest astrological text we have is called the 'Venus Tables of Amisaduqa' compiled during the reign of King Amisaduqa of Babylon, c. 1650BCE. Astrology in those times was generally 'mundane' – that is, it charted the fates of nations and rulers. In the final 600 years BCE astrology developed rapidly, and the first individual horoscope appeared at about 400BCE, shortly after the first use of the signs of the zodiac.

It is from the Greeks that astrology seems to have inherited its philosophic depth, beginning with Pythagoras of Samos c. 600BCE. Pythagoras is well known for his contribution to mathematics, but he was perhaps one of the most influential scholars of all time, and one of the most brilliant. The Pythagoreans were a mystical order who sought states of transcendence, and Pythagoras held that numbers expressed a quality as well as a quantity – for example, two represents duality, three creative harmony 'as Mother, Father, Child' and so on. This belief is central to the interpretation of astrological charts to this day. After Pythagoras many Greek astronomers put forward theories and refinements regarding the nature of the cosmos and solar system.

Astrology was practised throughout the known world, from Egypt through India and China. The Romans incorporated astrology into their systems, although the authorities were never totally comfortable with the subject. The notable figure of Claudius Ptolemy emerges from Alexandria. Born in 70CE, Ptolemy is remembered for his two textbooks, called the *Almagest* and the *Tetrabiblos*, which were used for the next 1,500 years. Through the 'dark ages' much astrological lore was preserved in Islamic countries, but in the fifteenth century astrology grew in popularity in the West. Queen Elizabeth I had her own personal astrologer, John Dee, and such fathers of modern astronomy as Kepler and Galileo served as court astrologers in Europe.

As the 'Age of Reason' dawned over Europe people embraced the Cartesian doctrine 'I think, therefore I am'. The human race began to believe it had grown up, adopting logic as the only means to explain life. However, astrology was taught at the University of Salamanca until 1776. What is rarely appreciated is that some of our greatest scientists, notably Newton and even Einstein, were led to their discoveries by intuition. Newton was a true mystic, and it was the search for meaning – the same motivation that inspired the Palaeolithic observer – that gave rise to some of our most brilliant advances. Indeed Newton is widely believed to have been an astrologer. The astronomer Halley, who discovered the famous comet, is reported to have criticised Newton for this, whereupon Sir Isaac replied 'I have studied it Sir, you have not!'

During the twentieth century astrology enjoyed a revival, and in 1948 The Faculty of Astrological Studies was founded, offering tuition of high quality and an examination system. The great psychologist Carl Jung was a supporter of astrology, and his work has expanded ideas about the mythic connections of the birth chart. Astrology is still eyed askance by many people, and there is no doubt that there is little purely scientific corroboration for astrology – an exception to this is the exhaustive statistical work undertaken by the Gauquelins. Michel Gauquelin was a French statistician whose research shows undeniable connection between professional prominence and the position of planets at birth. Now that the concept of a mechanical universe is being superseded, there is a greater chance that astrology and astronomy will reunite.

Notwithstanding the lack of statistical support, anyone who consults a good astrologer comes away deeply impressed by the insight of the birth chart. Often it is possible to see very deeply into the dynamics of the personality and to be able to throw light on current dilemmas. It is noteworthy that even the most sceptical of people tend to know their Sun sign and the characteristics associated with it.

## ■ WHAT IS A BIRTH CHART?

Your birth chart is a map of the heavens drawn up for the time, date and place of your birth. An astrologer will prefer you to be as accurate as you can about the time of day, for that affects the sign rising on the eastern horizon. This 'rising sign' is very important to your personality. However, if you do not know your birth time a chart can still be compiled for you. There will be some details

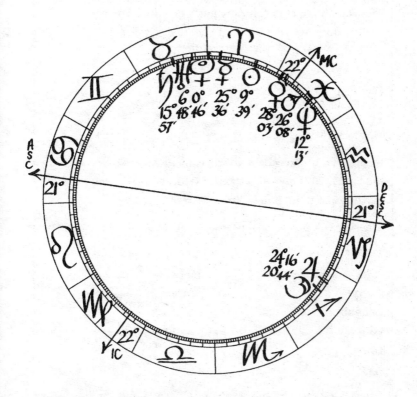

**The birth chart of Vincent Van Gogh**
Vincent has Sun ☉ and Mercury ☿ in Aries ♈. However, Venus ♀, Mars ♂ and Neptune ♆ are in Pisces ♓, thus intensifying his sensitivity, which is further emphasised by Cancer ♋ on the Ascendant.

missing, but useful interpretations may still be made. It is far better for the astrologer to know that your birth time is in question than to operate from a position of false certainty. The birth chart for Vincent Van Gogh, above, is a simplified chart. Additional factors would be entered on the chart and considered by an astrologer, such as angles (aspects) between the planets, and the houses.

The **planets** are life principles, energy centres. To enable you to understand the birth chart, here are their glyphs:

| | | | |
|---|---|---|---|
| Sun | ☉ | Jupiter | ♃ |
| Moon | ☽ | Saturn | ♄ |
| Mercury | ☿ | Uranus | ♅ |
| Venus | ♀ | Neptune | ♆ |
| Mars | ♂ | Pluto | ♇ (ᴘ) |

**Rising Sign** or **Ascendant** (**ASC**) is the way we have of meeting the world, our outward persona. **Midheaven** (**MC**) refers to our image, aspirations, how we like to be seen.

The **signs** are modes of expression, ways of being. Here are their glyphs:

| | | | |
|---|---|---|---|
| Aries | ♈ | Libra | ♎ |
| Taurus | ♉ | Scorpio | ♏ |
| Gemini | ♊ | Sagittarius | ♐ |
| Cancer | ♋ | Capricorn | ♑ |
| Leo | ♌ | Aquarius | ♒ |
| Virgo | ♍ | Pisces | ♓ |

Using knowledge of the glyphs you can see that the Sun is in Aries in our example birth chart (page 5).

The birth chart shows each of the planets and the Moon in the astrological signs, and can be thought of as an 'energy map' of the different forces operating within the psyche. Thus the Sun sign (often called 'birth sign' or 'star sign') refers only to the position of the Sun. If the planets are in very different signs from the Sun sign, the interpretation will be greatly modified. Thus, if a person has Sun in Leo yet is somewhat introverted or quiet, this may be because the Moon was in reserved Capricorn when that person was born. Nonetheless, the Sun represents the light of consciousness, the integrating force, and most people recognise that they are typical of their Sun sign, although in some people it will be more noticeable than in others. The planets Mercury and Venus are very close to the Sun and often occupy the same sign, so intensifying the Sun-sign influence.

This book is written about your Sun sign, because the Sun sign serves as an accessible starting point for those wishing to learn about themselves through astrology. However, do not let your interest stop there. If you find anything helpful in comments and advice stemming from Sun sign alone, you will find your true birth chart even more revealing. The address of the Faculty of Astrological Studies appears in 'Further Reading and Resources' at the back of this book, and it is a good idea to approach them for a list of trained astrologers who can help you. Moon *phase* at birth (as distinct from Moon sign) is also very important. *The Moon and You for Beginners* (see 'Further Reading') explains this fascinating area clearly, and provides a simple chart for you to look up your Moon phase, and learn what this means for your personality.

## ■ HOW DOES ASTROLOGY WORK?

We cannot explain astrology by the usual methods of cause and effect. In fact, there are many things we cannot explain. No one can define exactly what life is. We do not know exactly what electricity is, but we know how to use it. Few of us have any idea how a television set works, but we know how to turn it on. Although we are not able to explain astrology we are still able to use it, as any capable astrologer will demonstrate.

Jung discovered something called 'synchronicity'. This he defined as 'an acausal connecting principle'. Simply, this means that some events have a meaningful connection *other than cause and effect*. The planets do not cause us to do things, but their movements are synchronistic with our lives. The old dictum 'as above, so below' applies here. It is a mystery. We can't explain it, but that doesn't mean we should refuse to believe in it. A little boy on a visit to the circus saw an elephant for the first time and said 'There's no such thing'. We may laugh at the little boy, but how many of us respond to things we do not understand in this way?

The planetary positions in your birth chart are synchronistic with the time of your birth, when you took on separate existence, and they are synchronistic with your individuality in this life. They have much to say about you.

## ■ MYTH AND PSYCHOLOGY

The planets are named after the old gods and goddesses of Rome, which in turn link in with Greek and other pantheons. The planets represent 'life principles' – forces that drive the personality, and as such they can be termed 'archetypal'. This means that they are basic ideas, universal within human society and are also relevant in terms of the forces that, in some inexplicable way, inhabit the corners of the universe and inform the Earth and all human institutions. Thus the assertive energy that is represented by Mars means energetic action of all sorts – explosions and fires, wars, fierce debates and personal anger. Put briefly, here are the meanings of the planets:

- Mercury – intellect and communication
- Venus – love, unifying, relating
- Mars – assertion, energy, fighting spirit
- Jupiter – expansion, confidence, optimism
- Saturn – limitation, discipline
- Uranus – rebellion, independence

- Neptune – power to seek the ideal, sense the unseen
- Pluto – power to transform and evolve

These principles are modified according to the astrological sign they inhabit; thus Venus in Pisces may be gently loving, dreamy and self-sacrificing, while Venus in Aries will be demanding and adventurous in relationships. Thus the planets in signs form a complex psychological framework – and that is only part of the story of chart interpretation!

In the old mythologies these 'energies' or 'archetypes' or 'gods' were involved in classical dramas. An example is the story of Saturn and Uranus. Uranus is the rejecting father of Saturn, who later castrates and murders his father – thus innovative people reject reactionaries, who then murder them; so the revolutionary part of the personality is continually 'killed off' by the restrictive part. The exact positions and angles between the planets will indicate how this and other myths may come to life. In addition, the mere placement of planets by sign – and, of course, especially the Sun sign, call forth various myths as illustrations. The ancient myths are good yarns, but they are also inspired and vivid dramatisations of what may be going on repeatedly within your personality and that of your nearest and dearest. Myths are used by many modern psychologists and thera-pists in a tradition that has grown since Jung. We shall be using mythic themes to illustrate internal dynamics in this book.

# ■ THE SIGNS OF THE ZODIAC

There are twelve signs, and each of these belongs to an Element – Earth, Fire, Air or Water, and a Quality – Cardinal, Fixed or Mutable. The Cardinal signs are more geared to action, the Fixed tend to remain stable and rooted, whereas the Mutable signs are adaptable, changeable.

| SIGN | QUALITY | ELEMENT |
|------|---------|---------|
| Aries | Cardinal | Fire |
| Taurus | Fixed | Earth |
| Gemini | Mutable | Air |
| Cancer | Cardinal | Water |
| Leo | Fixed | Fire |
| Virgo | Mutable | Earth |
| Libra | Cardinal | Air |
| Scorpio | Fixed | Water |
| Sagittarius | Mutable | Fire |
| Capricorn | Cardinal | Earth |
| Aquarius | Fixed | Air |
| Pisces | Mutable | Water |

Jung defined four functions of consciousness – four different ways of perceiving the world – 'thinking', 'feeling', 'sensation' and 'intuition'. Thinking is the logical, evaluative approach that works in terms of the mind. Feeling is also evaluative, but this time in relation to culture and family needs. This is not the same as emotion, although 'feeling' people often process emotions more smoothly than other types. Jung saw 'feeling' as rational, too. 'Sensation' refers to the 'here and now', the five physical senses, while 'intuition' relates to the possible, to visions and hunches. Jung taught that we tend to have one function uppermost in consciousness, another one or maybe two secondary and another repressed or 'inferior', although we all possess each of these functions to some degree.

Jungian ideas are being refined and expanded, and they are incorporated into modern methods of personality testing, as in the Myers-Briggs test. If a prospective employer has recently given you such a test, it was to establish your talents and potential for the job. However, the basic four-fold division is still extremely useful, and I find that it is often of great help in assisting clients to understand themselves, and their partners, in greater depth – for we are all apt to assume that everyone processes information and applies it in the same way as we do. But they don't! It is worthy of mention that the important categories of 'introverted' and 'extraverted' were also identified by Jung. In astrology, Fire and Air signs seem to be extraverted, generally speaking, and Earth and Water introverted – and this has been borne out by the statistical research of the astrologer, Jeff Mayo. However, this doesn't mean that all feeling and sensation people are introverted and all intuitives and thinkers extraverted – this is definitely not the case, and calls for more detailed examination of the chart (e.g. lots of Fire and Water may mean an extravert feeling type).

Very broadly speaking we may link the Fire signs to intuition, Water to feeling, Earth to sensation and Air to thinking. Often thinking and feeling are drawn together and sensation and intuition are attracted, because they are opposites. This probably happens because we all seek to become whole, but the process can be painful. The notion of the four functions, when understood, does help to throw light on some of the stumbling blocks we often encounter in relationships. However, some people just do not seem to fit. Also Fire doesn't always correspond to intuition, Water to feeling, etc. – it seems this is usually the case, but not all astrologers agree. Some link Fire with feeling, Water with intuition, and most agree that other chart factors are also important. As with all theories, this can be used to help, expand and clarify, not as a rigid system to impose definitions. We shall be learning more about these matters in relation to the Sun sign in following pages.

# ■ THE PRECESSION OF THE EQUINOXES

One criticism often levelled at astrology is that 'the stars have moved' and so the old signs are invalid. There is some truth in this, and it is due to a phenomenon called 'The Precession of the Equinoxes'. The beginning of the sign Aries occurs when the Sun is overhead at the equator, moving northwards. This is called the Spring Equinox, for now day and night are equal all over the globe, and the first point of Aries is called the 'equinoctial point'. Because the Earth not only turns on its axis but 'rocks' on it (imagine a giant knitting needle driven through the poles – the Earth spins on this, but the head of the needle also slowly describes a circle in space) the 'equinoctial point' has moved against the background of stars. Thus, when the Sun is overhead at the equator, entering Aries, it is no longer at the start of the constellation of Aries, where it occurred when the signs were named, but is now in the constellation of Pisces. The 'equinoctial point' is moving backwards into Aquarius, hence the ideas of the dawning 'Aquarian age'.

So where does that leave astrology? Exactly in the same place, in actuality. For it all depends on how you think the constellations came to be named in the first place. Did our ancestors simply look up and see the shape of a Ram in the sky? Or did they – being much more intuitive and in tune with their surroundings than we are – feel sharply aware of the quality, the energies around at a certain time of the year, and *then* look skyward, translating what they sensed into a suitable starry symbol? This seems much more likely – and you have only to look at the star groups to see that it takes a fair bit of imagination to equate most of them with the figures they represent! The Precession of the Equinoxes does not affect astrological interpretation, for it is based upon observation and intuition, rather than 'animals in the sky'.

# ■ USING THIS BOOK

*Reach Your Potential – Aries* explores your Sun sign and what this means in terms of your personality; the emphasis is on self-exploration. All the way through, hints are given to help you to begin to understand yourself better, ask questions about yourself and use what you have to maximum effect. This book will show you how to use positive Arien traits to your best advantage, and how to neutralise negative Arien traits. Don't forget that by reading it you are consenting, however obliquely, to the notion that you are connected in strange and mysterious ways to the web of the cosmos. What happens within you is part of a meaningful pattern that you can explore and become conscious of, thereby acquiring greater influence on the course of your life. Let this encourage you to ask further questions.

### Some famous Ariens

Marlon Brando, Nikita Krushchev, Harry Houdini, Vincent Van Gogh, Howard Sasportas (well-known astrologer), Leonard Nimoy (Mr Spock from Star Trek), Jeffrey Archer, Bette Davis, Julie Christie, John Major, Michael Heseltine, Clare Francis.

As women are poorly represented in this list, let us include the revolutionary and memorable dancer, Isadora Duncan who had Moon and Ascendant in Aries, and the prolific romantic novelist, Barbara Cartland who also has Moon and Ascendant in Aries. Sarah Ferguson, Duchess of York, has Moon in Aries and the actress Meryl Streep has an Aries Midheaven.

Naturally the fiery energies and dynamism of any Arien influence are a great help in the competitive world of public life, the creative demands of the arts and the rough and tumble of politics.

# Ram, Rambo or Hero – what sort of Aries are you?

Here is a quiz to give an idea of how you are operating at the moment. Its tone is light hearted, but the intent is serious, and you may learn something about yourself. Don't think too hard about the answers, just pick the one that appeals most to you.

1. **Your host or hostess asks if you would like tea or coffee. You respond:**

   a) ☐ 'Yes', feeling impatient of the question. She should know what you like by now.

   b) ☐ 'Whatever is easiest.' You really don't mind and are oblivious to the fact that the other person would truly be happier if you chose.

   c) ☐ Your mind is ranging ahead to the prospect of a walk together on the sunlit hills/a stimulating conversation/ some wonderful lovemaking. Observing that coffee will be quickest, you go for that.

2. **Arriving at a restaurant with your best friend or lover, you find your table has not been reserved, despite the call you made earlier. How do you react?**

   a) ☐ Shout angrily, so that everyone in the packed dining room can hear, demanding a solution.

   b) ☐ Argue determinedly in a clipped, inflexible manner that this isn't good enough, and what are they going to do about it.

   c) ☐ Suggest the management supply you and your friend with a drink or two on the house, while you make free use of their telephone to arrange a suitable alternative for the evening.

**3. You are feeling depressed – what happens now?**

**a)** ☐ You never get depressed, it's just other people who annoy you.

**b)** ☐ You're never really depressed (heaven forbid you should admit to it!).

**c)** ☐ You're quite happy to seek therapy and admit you hate your mother or want to murder your father, if that is true. But you want a quick answer and to find out what to do about it – life's too short to be in the doldrums, and you want to get on with it.

**4. A charity collector approaches you for a donation. This happens to be for a cause you do not wish to support, or have heard is questionable. So you:**

**a)** ☐ Are rude and even abusive to the collector, who should know better than to work for something like that – such people are a menace.

**b)** ☐ You simply refuse.

**c)** ☐ You explain firmly and clearly why you will not support the cause.

**5. New neighbours move in next door and their music pounds through the wall causing considerable disturbance until the small hours. What do you do?**

**a)** ☐ Stride round in your dressing gown and threaten to rip out their speakers and wrap them around their necks – you mean it!

**b)** ☐ Bang loudly on the wall and put your own music on, full blast, at 6 a.m,, when you hope they are asleep.

**c)** ☐ After enduring one night of disturbance you call on them next evening, explaining how they have disturbed you and asking them not to repeat it.

6. **Your lover is upset with you – you have forgotten a birthday/anniversary or not been supportive enough at a critical time. How do you put matters right?**

   a) ☐ You're not really quite sure what you've done and anyway your lover is far too sensitive. You act irritable and offish. Many of your relationships may have ended there.

   b) ☐ You try a clumsy apology followed by breezy attempts to take your lover's mind off it all.

   c) ☐ Realising that only dramatic remedies will save the situation, you respond with a deluge of roses or an impromptu trip in a hot-air balloon, complete with champagne in mid-flight. Or, if you're hard up, you try offering a poem on bended knee (perhaps in black underwear, for female Ariens).

7. **At work you submit a brilliant and relevant report, and are surprised that it has been ignored. Later you find your boss has implemented your proposals as his or her own, so you:**

   a) ☐ Stamp into the MD's office, insult the company and slap down your resignation, scratching the mahogany desktop as you go.

   b) ☐ You act sullen, coming in late and complaining loudly about cheats within earshot of your boss.

   c) ☐ You request a private word with your boss and state openly how you feel.

8. **You have your indicator on for that convenient parking space when a Mini comes from the other side and nips straight in to it.**

   a) ☐ Flying into a rage you back your bumper against the Mini revving up and shouting.

   b) ☐ You blow your horn and shake your fist before moving on.

   c) ☐ You park temporarily and give the usurper a few home truths.

9. **The unthinkable is happening. Just as you and your lover are getting carried away there is a footstep on the stairs. You know that it is the parents (or worse, the spouse) come home early, and you are caught.**

   **a)** ☐ Telling yourself 'death before dishonour' you launch yourself from the window – after all, that branch looks as if it will take your weight.

   **b)** ☐ Deciding the wardrobe isn't big enough to hide in, you begin thinking up excuses.

   **c)** ☐ You know there is no escape and the time has come to face the consequences. Grabbing clothes and as much dignity as possible you prepare to face the music.

Now count up your score. What do you have most of – a's, b's or c's?

**Mostly a's.** Well, you're a Rambo all right, or at least that is the phase you are going through at present. You have energy and the courage of your convictions, but little subtlety. If you can develop a bit of forethought (I know that's not easy) and become more conscious of the fact there are other people in the world besides yourself, you will truly be a force to be reckoned with. You can achieve much.

**Mostly b's.** You are a typical Ram – a bit thoughtless, impetuous and fiery. You have masses of energy and you can learn to put your talents to good use, to become truly effectual.

**Mostly c's.** You really are a Hero, always facing up to situations, asserting yourself when and where you should and making good use of your imagination. Do remember that not everyone on the planet can match up to your standards and maybe you can still learn about subtlety.

If you found that in many cases none of the answers seemed anywhere near to fitting you, then it may be that you are an uncharacteristic Aries. This may be because there are factors in your astrological chart that inhibit the expression of your Sun sign, or it may be because there is a preponderance of other signs, outweighing the Aries part. Whatever the case may be, your Sun-sign potential needs to be realised. Perhaps you will find something to help ring a few bells in the following pages.

# 1 ♈ The essential Aries

*Boldness, and again boldness, and always boldness*

Danton, Speech to French Legislative Committee, 2 September, 1792

## ■ HEAD FIRST – AND DEVIL TAKE THE HINDMOST

Aries people tend to get themselves noticed and you are often easy to spot simply from the way you move. You have a tendency to thrust your head forwards and to let the rest of the body follow as it may, and your centre of gravity seems always ahead of you. Even the more stately Aries – and there are a few – will have their hosts on the edge of their seats as they gesticulate enthusiastically, centimetres from a full coffee cup. 'Careful,' they try to warn Aries, smiling and pointing. Too late – there is the coffee all over their new carpet. Now they had better be quick, for Aries will leap up to get a cloth and matters will go from bad to worse as they avidly rub the spillage further into the fibres!

At this point Aries readers may well grin goodhumouredly, but some of you may wonder if you have been branded the clumsy oaf of the zodiac. Not so! It is the sheer energy of Aries, the exuberance and zest for life that can cause blundering, for when Aries is focussed in suitable activity you are precision itself, with all the grace of a javelin in full flight.

Because you are often very intent upon your goals, you do not always notice what is close by, and that can make for accidents and upsets. However, because of your single-mindedness you have the potential to be an achiever, of the first order.

## The Myth of the Ram

Greek legend tells how King Athamas of Boeotia loved the cloud queen Nephele and had two children by her, Phrixus and Helle. Their stepmother, Ino, conspired to have them sacrificed to restore fertility to the earth, which she herself had parched. However, a magical winged ram with golden fleece rescued them – presumably sent by their celestial mother. Helle became dizzy and fell off into the Hellespont – so called in her honour. Helle has connections with more ancient goddesses of tide and Moon. Meanwhile Phrixus went on to Colchis and sacrificed the ram to Zeus, who placed its likeness in the heavens.

Later on, the golden fleece becomes the subject of a brave quest by the hero Jason, who is a very Arien figure. The princess Medea, a magical adept, falls in love with the hero, and helps him to steal the fleece, displaying a cruel ruthlessness which she later turns on the faithless Jason, for she kills all their children and rides off in a chariot drawn by serpents, leaving her errant spouse to an aimless, empty life. Jason, brought low, slumps in self-pity beneath the rotting hulk of his once magnificent ship, the *Argo*. There he is killed, his brains dashed out by a piece of falling wood.

This tale has several points of relevance. Medea is a very Scorpionic figure, and it may warn of the potential problems between the two signs! In Jason we see the best and the worst of Aries, for he is resourceful and indomitable. However, he is also arrogant. He forgets whence his help has come and he neglects the domain of relationships and emotions. Eventually he becomes aimless because he is not 'earthed'. Without wife and family, too old to be a hero any longer, his life ends with an injury to which many Ariens are prone – a blow to the head!

Myths are not, of course, intended to be taken literally, and it is far more inspiring for us to think of the shining golden fleece and how it reflects the verve and magnificence of Aries. The Ram is also an animal sacred to the ancient Mother Goddess, and its spiralling horns signify transcendence and the transition between the world of potential and the world of manifestation – very much as Arien theme.

## ■ ELEMENT, QUALITY AND RULING PLANET

We have seen that each of the signs of the zodiac belongs to one of the Elements, Earth, Fire, Air or Water, and one of the Qualities, Cardinal, Fixed or Mutable. Aries is Cardinal Fire. This means that Aries folk are action oriented and fiery. However, 'fiery' in this case doesn't necessarily mean hot tempered and volatile (although in the case of Aries it might well!). A deeper meaning is concerned with the real nature of Fire, for this is a transformative Element, of pure energy. Flames leap and die, almost as if they come from another dimension, and this tells us something about Fire-sign people, in that they live in the world of the possible rather than the actual, they are vibrant with ideas, they inhabit the future – or maybe the past – but rarely the present. Sometimes it seems they can see around corners. They will follow hunches and take risks, but they may not stay to harvest what they plant. All these characteristics are strongly marked in Aries.

We have also seen that the element of Fire has some things in common with what Jung called the 'intuitive' function. This idea of intuition isn't quite the same as the 'gut feelings' that many Earth- or Water-sign people get, or the sort of idea that Air-sign people 'pick up on the ether', nor can it be dismissed as being airy-fairy. Rather it is a perception of life that projects consciousness into the future and lives by inspiration and vision. The Aries child making model planes in the bedroom looks no different to an average Taurus or Capricorn, and an Aries plumber can connect pipes as well as the next person. But the inner dynamics are different. For you Ariens there is always a Grand Scheme, even if this exists only deep within your soul. This dull old world is not always kind to fiery people, and many of you will choose to tell yourselves you are being purely practical. Indeed you may convince yourselves as well as others that this is true, but this is only skin deep.

Aries is the first sign of the zodiac, beginning the astrological year at the Spring Equinox. This implies a comment on the Arien nature, for you are pioneers, bursting upon the world with all the vibrancy and innocence of the greening time. However, for those of you who live in the Southern Hemisphere, Aries comes after the Autumn Equinox, preparing the way for winter. So you may prefer to think in terms of the clearing out of decaying life to usher the way into new patterns, for we all start to think differently as autumn sets in.

Each sign is said to have a 'Ruling Planet'. This means that there is a planet that has a special affinity with the sign, whose energies are most at home when expressed in terms of that sign. The Ruling Planet for Aries is Mars. Mars is the 'red planet', named after the Roman god of war. The god Mars was efficiently combative – a superb, ruthless warrior. We must not deduce from this that Aries is pugnacious, for many of our ways of perceiving are built upon a patriarchal, hierarchical and aggressive model. Mars fits this all too well. However, the keynote here is assertiveness. We are often told that extreme aggression or submission are two sides of the same coin and that true self-assertiveness is the healthy state to aim for. Aries, at best embodies beautiful, pure assertion of self, and there is something about this that affirms the individuality of everyone else, also. When accepted for themselves, Ariens can be liberating companions.

# ◼ HEROES AND HEROINES

There is something deeply heroic about the Arien approach to life.
You are not interested in half measures, and even if part of you may
wish for a comfortable compromise, such as favoured by your zodiacal opposite, Libra, you are not able to allow yourself this. It would
be a betrayal, a cop-out, and Arien instincts in such matters are
strong. When this is a question of which is the quickest way to get to
the local pub, Arien insistence can be irritating, to say the least.
However, in the days of knights and dragons, or the possible times
to come of Star Wars and Darth Vader, all may be grateful to have a
true Aries by their side. In our times, many Ariens may be found
taking risks in business, enterprises and creativity of all kinds.
Generally, your mission is to expand human experience, in some
form or fashion.

Aries is a champion, and it is important for you to have a cause and
to feel that you are spearheading some Grand Plan. Issue the average Aries with a challenge and there will be a response that may
make the challenger think a match has been set to a roman candle!
Aries wants to break new ground, to do something big, something
significant. Sometimes Aries people relish physical danger, yearning to go sky diving, bungee jumping or fire fighting. Others are
drawn more to intellectual, quieter pursuits. There may be no raz-
zamatazz at all, but the same kinds of things are going on inside. In
either case you may be strongly competitive, and it is characteristic
of Aries to love to feel you have done well, and to capitalise on your
achievements (unless you have messed up badly, in which case –
tragedy!).

The underlying need in Aries is not to feel you are The Best and to
grind all the competition into the ground. There is nothing
destructive or brutal about you generous, hot-headed folk. It is a
very basic drive in Aries to push back frontiers and to 'boldly go

where no one has gone before' for only by doing this do you feel alive, come to know yourself and experience your individuality. Aries people are enterprising, brave and resourceful, and you are born leaders. You are kind and warm-hearted champions of the underdog, and your energy and impulsiveness is second to none. Yes, you may be rash or impatient at times. You may seem unaware of the feelings of others, and have been accused of arrogance and self-will, but, lets face it, if you're fighting a dragon you can't be turning round to see whose toes you're treading on!

The point here is that you are fighting your own dragon, and this may be the 'dragon' of lack of consciousness in self or in others, it may be ignorance, prejudice, cruelty, or it may be something as pretty as being short changed by a dime or a penny in the grocery store. We may think of anything that suggests fighting as thoroughly bad, from our experience of World Wars and our fears of global conflict, muggings and gang violence, but we must not forget the noble impulse to strive onwards and to protect the vulnerable. The champion consciousness can't be switched on and off. Some battles do need to be fought by aspiring humankind, and someone has to fight them. If you have the guts to defend the weak, stick by your ideas or forge new conceptual frameworks you may choose to stand up in smaller matters also. Think how good you feel when you have risen to a challenge in your own chosen sphere and how strong a sense of your own identity this gives you. Those non-Ariens who are close to you can feel the warmth from your glowing eyes when you exclaim 'Yes! I *did* it!'.

From the foregoing it will be obvious that the image of Aries does not sit comfortably with the traditional idea of femininity – but here we have heroines as well as heroes. It is just as compatible with the female psyche to be assertive, to follow visions and to stand your ground as it is with the masculine – remember the Amazons, Joan of Arc and Boadicea? In ancient times Celtic women went into battle, fighting alongside the men. Women can bring a gentler, but no less passionate and committed, ambiance to the Arien spirit. Perhaps we see here a suggestion of the native American Rainbow Warrior, whom prophecy tells us will come to defend the Earth and her creatures.

## ■ COUNTING YOUR TOES

From speaking of the heroic quality of Aries we turn now to a quite different aspect. Aries can be most childlike. Of course, this does not mean childish, for you are as mature as the next person. However, there is in Aries a quality of self-absorption and innocence. Your inner purpose in life is to learn about yourself and experience all that is available, just in the way a baby does. Babies are fascinated by their own bodies, their growing powers and possibilities, and this endearing quality is often in evidence in Aries, but it can make you very vulnerable.

Do not let that enterprise and energy fool you into thinking that you can't be hurt, for you may be, and very deeply. Occasionally this may be because you haven't noticed someone standing in your path and, having got up again, that person lashes back. You are mortally wounded, because you *really* didn't notice the other person. More frequently, however, it may be that you have aroused jealousy, resentment or opposition, or it may just be the ordinary course of life that deals its blows. If a toddler skins his knee a quick cuddle can put things right, but this is not always so for Aries, and many of you will go off to lick your wounds in private, desolate, lonely and uncomprehending. If you recognise yourself here, you may need to remind yourself that having the courage to seek the correct help may be the bravest action of all. There is no reason why you should feel you must shoulder all burdens, and it may be time for you to champion yourself. Those who love an Aries should recognise this vulnerability, but be very careful how they offer help, for the Arien pride is ferocious and may be self-destructive.

## ■ PRACTICAL – OR KNOT?

Many Aries people have a reputation for being practical. This probably stems from the fact that you are active and if there is a problem, from a philosophical conundrum to a car that won't start, your impulse is to sort it out. Because of your determination and resourcefulness, many of you are successful at putting up shelves, landscaping the garden and feeding the 5,000 – but don't be fooled! Every Aries secretly knows that the world of Things is a wholesale conspiracy to frustrate, confuse, threaten and disappoint.

As a Fire sign, you are likely to be 'intuitive'. What is truly real to you is the domain of the potential rather than the actual. Ideas, visions, plans, possibilities – these are the Arien currency. Culturally, we value the down-to-earth, and because of this most Ariens, who are nothing if not enterprising, pick up the baton of practicality and run with it. In so doing you trip over wires and steps, lose your car keys (locked in the boot again) and never quite have the right size of screw or nail. Never mind, you win through in the end, and your house will probably fall down before the picture that you have just spent an hour attaching to the wall.

Because you are not really at home with Things (though many would die rather than admit to it) some of you make a profession out of complaining. In this you are more persistent, resourceful and vehement than any Virgo – reputed to be the fussiest sign of all – would ever dare to be. The world is going to wrack and ruin, things ain't what they used to be, and heroic Aries is going to restore Utopia single handed. Hapless waiters or bus-drivers may find themselves the windmill that Aries decides to tilt at – and that's not a comfortable position! However, it is really Aries that suffers in these matters. Slowly, inexorably, you may find that you are enmeshed in a web of your own making, fussing about nothing and going nowhere, rather like the laboratory spiders, injected with caffeine, whose webs were chaotic and hopelessly inefficient.

If you are an Aries and you recognise this, why not give yourself permission to do what you'd really like to do, instead of tying yourself in knots? Remember the myth of the Gordian knot? This is the story.

## The Gordian Knot

Many years ago the people of Gordium, a town near Ankara in Turkey, were told by an oracle that the first man who came to them in a wagon should be king. This turned out to be a peasant called Gordius, and when he was crowned he dedicated his wagon to Jupiter. Thereafter it was believed that the man who could untie the knot which attached the yolk of the wagon to the pole would rule all Asia. In the year 333BCE Alexander the Great came to Gordium. Hearing the prophecy he scorned to fumble with the knot, but slashed straight through it with his sword.

So why not cut through your own version of the Gordian Knot, when occasion demands? What would you really like to try, where would you like to be? What ambitions do you truly cherish – never mind how wild or silly they may seem (or someone, way back in the past, told you they were). Set yourself free. Faith in your own capabilities is very important to you, and if you are being pernickety it may be because you have lost some of that faith. Try to reclaim it.

## ◼ THE BIG SULK

Occasionally there may be an Aries who seems to embody none of the enthusiasm, courage and energy that are characteristic of this sign. This Aries has shoulders hunched, lips sagging in a pout – an invisible cloud seems to be hanging around the brow and it may be almost impossible to be positive, encouraging or even moderately active.

This is a real tragedy, for here is an Aries caught in the negative side of the sign, in a childlike petulance. If this is you, your problem really is frustrated rage. Somewhere down the line all your natural élan has been repressed or knocked out of you. You want to be a child again – a properly nurtured child this time – the world owes you a living, you want love, money and appreciation without doing anything to earn it (after all, a voice says deep within, aren't you *entitled?*) and you are just going to sit in that corner, exuding your own squidlike inkiness until 'Mum' comes to cajole you out of it.

### Achilles and Patroclus

There is a story told in the *Iliad* – the story of the Trojan wars – how the hero Achilles sulked in his tent, while his band of followers, the mighty Myrmidons, kicked their heels. This was because Achilles had been thwarted by King Agamemnon in his desire for the beautiful captive Briseis whom the king had claimed for himself. If Achilles couldn't have her, then he just wasn't going to fight, and that was that! Patroclus, his cousin who had long lived in Achilles' shadow, donned his armour and impersonated him. The Trojans, knowing their luck was in with Achilles out of the way, came down to burn the Greek ships, but Patroclus bravely put them to flight. Alas, his good fortune ran out. His helmet was torn off and as he staggered, blinded by a Trojan blow, a sword drove into his chest and he fell and died. All the Greeks rallied to protect the precious body, and it was thus

that Achilles came upon his beloved friend and mentor. In a storm of
rage and grief, Achilles' battle fever came upon him. Surrounded by
his Myrmidons he cut through the Trojan ranks, who retreated
before him like chaff in the wind. As the Sun sank over the scarlet
sea, and both sides counted their dead, Achilles picked up the corpse
of his dear friend and buried it on the shore. Swearing revenge on
Hector, who had killed his cousin, Achilles was back in action, but
brave Patroclus was now lost forever to the Land of Shades.

If you feel life had been unfair to you it may be hard to come out
and fight. Many Aries, regardless of life experience, may have the
sneaking feeling that life isn't really fair. It doesn't value you
enough, or give you the opportunities you merit and crave. It is true
that the intuitive fire of Aries isn't always valued, but let's face it, the
only one who can do anything about it is you! There really isn't any
other way. Do not wait for your own version of the loss of Patroclus.
If you can let it sink into your head and heart that no Big Mamma or
powerful patron is going to come and lift you out of your depres-
sion, that is the first step to doing something about it yourself.
Believe in yourself! In time you will come to appreciate that the universe really is a benevolent place, and you can find a special home as
the true child of the gods that you are.

The true Arien energy is about action and vision, and sometimes it
is because this is so essentially simple that it may be hard to accept –
people look for complications, not least Aries themselves. You will
do yourself a favour if you keep reminding yourself that life is about
forward motion, dreams, schemes and progress. The trick is to
temper this with a little realism and wisdom, not to stymie it with
resentment or needless complications.

## ■ PRACTICE AND CHANGE ■

- Trust your hunches where possible, they are likely to be right.
- Find a challenge – you just can't find your true self without it!
- Take risks sometimes. An Aries that is always cautious is an Aries whose flame is dampened.
- Do remember to seek help when you need it – you aren't invulnerable or omnipotent.
- Remember, although you can accomplish much, it is not up to you to sort out the world single handed.
- Be assertive, but be kind. Remember the times when you have felt bruised. Don't hurt others – it won't help you achieve your objective and you may need them at some time.

### Imagination

We have talked quite a lot in this chapter about the 'intuition' of Aries. Some of you may be puzzled by this. Isn't 'intuition' rather an insubstantial, 'iffy' sort of thing? What on earth are you supposed to do with it? It may be hard to integrate the idea of intuition with Arien enterprise and initiative.

I have tried to explain that intuition isn't about vague dreaminess. As an Aries you may be impatient with the idea of dreams, but you are a person of vision. You may be so used to acting on your inner feelings, 'shooting from the hip' that you don't really know you are doing it. You may have absorbed some dogma that reads 'wishing isn't any good', 'daydreams won't pay the bills'. If so, you may have buried alive the most vivid part of your nature. Your ability to dream dreams, to imagine, is your trump card.

Imagination doesn't mean being airy-fairy, spaced out, lost in some haze or fable. Imagination is the primary tool with which we create our world. All exists in the imagination before it takes shape in stone, on canvas, in metal, fabric or flesh.

Begin by giving yourself express permission to be imaginative. This doesn't mean disconnecting from everyday life at all, but it may mean envisioning it differently. What are your secret dreams? What sort of person would you really like to be? What is fencing you in, and why? Write down your thoughts, however crazy, and don't be afraid to follow ideas deep into uncharted mental territory. You are only playing with ideas now. What have you been told (or told yourself) you couldn't do, couldn't be, couldn't have? Is this really reasonable?

What about your daily life, job, leisure, relationships? Could you do things differently? How might a new approach enliven things, change them? What about risks? As an Aries you need to take risks – no, that doesn't mean placing your last pound or dollar on the favourite in the next race, but it means pushing the boat out a little somewhere, emotionally, conceptually, intellectually, financially. There are frontiers waiting for you to explore. You will find them by the light of your imagination.

# 2 Relationships

*To be wise and love
Exceeds man's might*

Shakespeare, *Troilus and Cressida*

To Aries all is larger than life on the most ordinary day. When Aries falls in love, the era of enchantment and magic has returned from the mists of time. There may be quests, mysteries and glittering treasures. All is glowing, all suggests hidden meanings, and the very earth trembles beneath the feet of the gods and goddesses that tread it, by sunlight and moonglow.

Sounds extreme? Well, even the most prosaic of us are aware how love can put a spring in our step, light in our life and add new meaning to what had become stale and empty. The sweet breath of love fans the flames of Arien ardour until all changes in this mighty alchemy – the earth really moves! To Aries all is infused with a significance beyond the ordinary. Prone to inflate the general importance of the day to day at the best of times, Aries in love becomes a knight of the Grail or a wild and daring adventuress, while the loved one takes on mythic significance.

If everyday life seems boring, people with a strong Aries content in their birth chart – it doesn't have to be just the Sun sign – may look elsewhere for their drama. She may be a nurse and he may be a computer engineer, but they knew each other in a former life when she was imprisoned by an evil lord in his tower, while he rode to save her on his white charger.

Of course, not all Ariens are absorbed in these delicious fantasies – although many are in the secret corners of their souls, if nowhere else. Aries may also react to emotion by intellectualising a little. This is not the Air-sign impulse to detachment. What you wish to do is to fit your feelings into a wider context. Some of you will take to philosophy, others will make plans, ask questions. Some will entertain the idea of a relationship that is quite prosaic, because you have been told, or told yourself that romance is silly, unreasonable and outdated. Aries can be quite cool about terminating a relationship that is impractical, through distance or some other obstacle, for you do not have the need for emotional intimacy that draws the hearts of the Water signs. The Water signs, especially Pisces, may also mythologise love, but theirs is usually a gentler, dreamier approach. Whatever the case, however, romance is there, waiting to cast its spell upon Aries. You may laugh, saying it hasn't got you yet, it's all nonsense and it's far more important for you to pass that exam, get that promotion, write that novel. You're ambitious, so you're not going to marry . . . . Maybe – but watch out! Some moonlit night you may get a whiff of that special narcotic and you'll be hooked. Nothing will ever be the same again!

## ■ ARIEN SEXUALITY

As you may imagine, Aries is a passionate sign and seeks to show love in the most physical ways. The male Aries may be a tireless and inventive lover – who says it all has to happen in the sack? You like new stimulus and you are adventurous and energetic sexually. No systematic working through of the *Kama Sutra* – you have quite enough imagination not to need any book, although one may occasionally be consulted, for extra inspiration. As a lover you seek to achieve ever greater heights for yourself and your partner, and to conjure into existence the true mystery of the erotic. As this can never quite be accomplished, you find here the challenge of an unreachable – but, tantalisingly, almost reachable quest.

## Male Aries

You may be getting the impression that Aries is an unstoppable lover and that no hint of doubt or insecurity ever permeated the Ram's loins, but you would be wrong. However physical and passionate Aries may be, yours is a Fire sign. The truth of the matter is that male Aries is not that comfortable with the physical body at all. For the male Aries, your best-kept secret is your insecurity and fear of impotence. This body thing just isn't to be relied on, and it's dreadful if your heart is full of derring-do and certain bits of you won't do anything! You may find yourself suddenly unable to have sex, and have no idea why. You will feel embarrassed and smitten with failure. How could this be? Nothing ever seemed more wonderful, and here you are, unable to perform – and performance is so important to you, in every sense of the word. I am afraid that some Aries men at this point do blame their partners. It is most unfair to blame a mortal woman for not being the goddess that you decided she was, and relationships may go awry here, leaving the woman especially scarred, because she isn't aware that the inadequacy isn't her own.

The crux of the matter is that Aries man expects too much – not only of other people and situations, but most especially of himself. The body has its own wisdom. Aries may refuse to be bound by ordinary constraints, including that of mortal flesh. However, the power and enigma of sexual love rests just upon its combination of emotional, spiritual and physical elements. If you can allow yourself to be fascinated by the process, instead of feeling crushed by your 'inadequacy' you may find yourself on a quest that is wonderful.

# The hero Cuchulain

The great Irish hero, Cuchulain, son of the Sun-god Lugh 'the shining one' was the most fearsome warrior ever known in Ireland. When his battle fever was upon him a geyser of bright blood spurted unendingly from his temple and live sparks issued from his mouth. Cuchulain's love for Emer of the flaming hair is well known in Irish myth, and stories tell of his fantastic battle prowess, using the salmon leap taught to him by the warrior-goddess Scathach in order to enter the castle of Emer's father and snatch his love from the mighty warriors that surrounded her.

Emer was the 'earthly' love of Cuchulain. Impulsive, proud and fearless, she was the equal of her husband in many respects and even made some of his life decisions for him. Both Emer and Cuchulain are rather 'Arien' in nature. However, Cuchulain's more spiritual essence is represented by the ethereal faery woman, Fand, who approached him by the devious guises of the Otherworld. At first Cuchulain was laid low by an enchanted wasting sickness and was unable to come to be with Fand, despite her love for him. For the sickness of Cuchulain was part of a 'breaking down' process, where he had to learn the limitations of his heroic approach in order to grow nearer to his spiritual self. Emer encouraged him to be with Fand at first, for she knew that a spell can be lifted only by the one who has cast it. However, at length her jealousy became too much for her, and she fiercely challenged Cuchulain and his faery lover, accompanied by her women, all armed with knives. Fand knew he belonged to Emer, and sadly she relinquished him, disappearing with her old lover, the sea god Manannan. For many a long day, Cuchulain pined for his faery woman, and Emer too grew pale in the knowledge Cuchulain had loved Fand as much as her, until at length the chief Druid gave them each a magic potion of forgetfulness to drink, and life went on as it had before.

Until his encounter with Fand Cuchulain is more of a 'Rambo' type, and it takes a year and a day, languishing on his sickbed, robbed of all his strength on which he had relied, for the hero to find the ability to enter another reality. However, having found this land of magic, it is hard to relinquish its beauty. A way must be found to return to ordinary life again, taking within one something of the secrets one has learned. With this in mind, perhaps Aries can learn to accept bodily limitations as a potential passage into a greater vision. We are all familiar with the theme of disability causing people to find their greatest talents, but perhaps the very small 'disability' of occasional impotence may be useful as a pointer to explore deeper – for the dimensions of love are limitless, as every Aries senses. Another point to the story is that, although some enchantment may be essential, it cannot become overwhelming, or Aries can be lost to 'ordinary' life, as Cuchulain was temporarily lost to Emer, and thus rendered ineffectual.

## Female Aries

Female Ariens are generally much more earthed than their male counterparts, and identify with their natural rhythms, as do all Fire-sign women. However, I have known Aries women who have said they feel sometimes as if their breasts don't belong to them, and they may find their periods especially inconvenient in an active lifestyle, where they prefer to be free. Female Aries may be a little 'iffy' about sex when it comes down to it – the idea is great and it all sounded very romantic by candlelight, and certainly you have lots of drive and desire. All would have been fine, if he hadn't blown his nose just then, or had remembered to take his socks off, but suddenly it's all a bit basic and that wild ardour cools a little.

# ■ ARIES WOMAN IN LOVE

This woman is prepared to give a great deal to her chosen mate. You will be a champion at his side in whatever battles life brings his way, you will look after him when he is ill and defend him savagely if he is attacked. If he is vulnerable you will protect him to the best of your considerable ability – and this will include intellectual, business, financial and creative matters as well as physical, for there is a Celtic warrior quality to many Aries ladies. What you won't do is respect him if he is weak. Aries knows well that weakness is not the same as sensitivity – in everyone else, that is. Within yourself, you may try very hard not to be sensitive, although you certainly are.

The Aries lady will willingly arm-wrestle (and you may win!), and you won't ask someone else to take off the tops of pickle jars. As a girl you were always wearing jeans and climbing trees with the boys, but as an adult you can wear high heels and stockings and vamp it up with the best, when necessary, for you are a sexy lady. You may even let a man open doors for you, in the interests of romance and style, but should a man ever patronise you, you will cut him down to size with a word or two from your razor-sharp tongue. If you slap his face it will be no hysterical flounder but a blow intended to black his eye!

When in love you are capable of giving and giving and giving. You have endless warmth and generosity. You are one of the 'rescuers' of the zodiac, and while the laurels for this usually go to Pisces, Aries will give help that is dynamic without a hint of the martyr. Not that you don't sometimes end up in a sad mess, however. One Aries lady I know managed to take up with a person perceived quite clearly by everyone else as a drunken, deceitful layabout. (Aries may be too innocent to appreciate the depths of human vice and may be overconfident in their ability to convert and remake – for many Ariens think they can change people.) This man prowled the house she shared with friends each night until the small hours, clutching bottles of whisky or gin, emptying the fridge and coming close to setting the house on fire. He lay in bed after she had gone to work, but arose at noon to shuffle off to the pub. Early afternoon gave him the opportunity to cut pages from her books and torture her cat. Added to this was the fact he was in love with another woman – he said so, on many occasions – and so avid had been his pursuit that that woman had to take out an injunction to keep him from pestering her.

After months of this, many women would have fled, forsaking job and property for some safety. Not so Aries. There were many tears and long examinations of his behaviour and extenuating circumstances, and her friends wondered how long this could possibly go on. They need not have worried. Enough was enough, and too much meant the time had come for action. One day while he was at the pub, out went his bag and baggage – through the window, naturally. The locks were changed and the police were informed that a former offender was 'at it again'. And that was that – sighs of relief all round. Would that all such tales might end so satisfactorily.

The Aries lady is is enduringly loyal, and while you don't suffer fools gladly, there is much you will suffer, in a good cause. Your feelings are strong and your heart can be easily broken. Often you find yourself drawn to men who are unobtainable, because they are so charismatic they are besieged by admirers, or they are homosexual, or married. But when you do choose someone suitable he should thank his lucky stars and get ready to build a dream.

## ■ ARIES MAN IN LOVE

With Aries we seem to talk a great deal about mythical heroes, knights, ladies and quests, and when it comes to the Aries man in love we are back in the courtly realms with a vengeance! You like to feel you have won a prize in the woman of your choice. You are not a comfortable companion for the ideological feminist, but if your lady doesn't mind letting you take the lead much of the time and if she is fairly secure in her own independence, she should bite her lip, conceal her smile and let you whirl her up in your arms and into a life of excitement.

Mr Aries does not spend his life swinging from castle ramparts with a box of chocolates under his arm. Most Aries – sadly for you - can't whisk their partner off by private jet to dinner in Paris, but some-where, somehow the scene is going to be rendered dramatic, even if it's only in words, hints, expressions, and at some point she is going to feel that you are players in a secret drama. At least, she's not quite sure it's *her* that's playing, precisely. You seem to be talking about her, but your eyes are fixed on the horizon, and she may begin casting around, wondering what she is supposed to say next.

One Aries man I knew, many years ago, was in love with a good friend of mine. She (as you might guess) was unavailable, having a committed relationship with someone else. How sorry I felt for Robert, and how romantic he appeared to my young eyes. Yes, I'll admit I did fancy him myself, but I knew it was no good. He had written my friend poetry and he was languishing – not in the dream-struck way of one who is wasting and 'palely loitering' but rather he had the desperate air of a man about to go off and join the Foreign Legion. We went for a walk out into the autumn wood-lands so he could unburden himself and talk of his plans.

The Sun came out and dappled the path, and Robert spoke ruefully about Jackie. We stopped in a patch of sunlight so that he could put all the force of his emotion behind his words.

'I know it's never going to happen,' he said. 'She sat there, smiling at Mike, and the sun turned her hair to pure gold – pure gold.' He was looking into the trees and I stood smiling at him, thinking how handsome he was. Then he looked at me, and something seemed to happen. The cameras had moved and were rolling again. Take two. Cue for Act Two, second heroine. I could almost hear the clapper-board.

'You've got lovely hair,' he said. 'It's really shiny and all coppery, tumbling down your back. Copper is the metal associated with Venus, you know.'

Now I bet you're thinking you know what happened next, but you'd be wrong! Flattered though I was, I did have some sense, and I thought more of myself than to allow myself to become a mere figment of someone's imagination. Making a hasty and embarrassed excuse, I hurried home, with him a few yards behind, no doubt rather bewildered, and avoided him thereafter. He didn't join any Legion. He married a local girl – not Jackie – and built up a successful business. As far as I know all is stable in his life to this day – outwardly, that is. Within I bet he still dreams those dreams and puts women on his pedestal to play his goddess, and I very much doubt if his wife understands him!

Robert is rather a two-dimensional example of a youthful Aries, but he does exemplify that element of fantasy that Aries man needs. You will build your partner into the woman of your dreams. That pedestal can be cramped and it's a long way down. You are also attracted to the unobtainable which can leave her in a Catch 22 situation if she loves you – and my, how lovable you are! It is important for a woman in love with Aries man always to hang on to her 'mystery' in some sense, and despite his rather domineering nature, submission is not the key to his heart – no way! That way lies boredom and a possible hasty exit, depending on circumstances.

The ardour of Aries is second to none and you are quite capable of being faithful when your heart is given – after all, 'undying love' is the courtly pledge. Life with you can never be dull, unless you are one of those Aries whose energies eat away at you internally, like acid, and even then you will manage to be interesting and graphic. Your lover should keep just a little of herself always to herself. You will walk by her side into the valley of death (as long as you get appreciated). You will give warmth, passion and commitment, all she could desire, and she will always know she is loved. She should leave you a corner in which to dream, and keep her own corner, too. You will support her with unflagging energy, but you don't really want to hear about her hormonal fluctuations or her worries that she may turn out to be like her mother. You may listen and answer inventively, but your heart will yearn for the mythical. So she must keep romance alive and keep a little of her independence. If she wants a little spice, a little adventure, then she's in the right place!

## ■ GAY ARIES

All remarks made above are relevant for the homosexuals of the sign – fantasy and romance are important elements in same-sex couples also. Tragically we know that life is not always easy for gay people. Aries, who are given to be trail blazers may 'come out' with a flourish, and may draw down all sorts of trouble upon their, no-doubt, already bruised heads. Other Aries, puzzled about their bodies at the best of times, may be deeply troubled about their homosexuality, feeling it shows they haven't got it 'quite right'. Remember, no one is more capable of love than you are, and the goddess says 'behold all acts of love and pleasure are my rituals' (a quotation from an invocation called 'The Charge'). Be gentle with yourself. Try to steer a middle course between blazoning it all from the rooftops or convulsing in self-doubt. Any form of loving is right, and your loving is a sacred expression of yourself.

## ■ ARIES LOVE TRAPS

### Falling in love with love

From the above it is not hard to see how it is the idea of love rather than the actuality that appeals to Aries, and what goes on isn't always about a real person, but about something happening inside your psyche. Being in love makes everything vibrant. It sharpens experience and gives glimpses of other dimensions. You thirst for the theatre of all of this for it makes life so much more meaningful and eventful. Unfortunately, taken to extremes, it is not a prelude to 'happy ever after' or anything like it. Many hearts can get broken with this approach, including yours. If you recognise yourself here, there are other ways to make life more exciting. Search for them in the physical and the spiritual. This may free you for the experience of a love that is real – and that could really blow your mind!

### The lure of the unattainable

Arthurian myth makes much of the long and thwarted passion between Lancelot and Guinevere. Sometimes it is agonising, this lack of consummation. One wonders why he doesn't just go off for good, make the break and seek fulfilment elsewhere. Or why he doesn't carry off his heroine and escape with her into the sunset. Truly this would be a daring deed worthy of Aries. Of course, it might seem dishonourable, which is anathema to a Fire sign, but at least it would be action. But no. All the action takes place in joust and combat, and while some stories tell of Lancelot's adultery with Guinevere and his rescue of her from the traitoress's pyre, we know there is no future for them, and we may be led to believe this is because of sin and disgrace – not so!

The tale of Arthur, Lancelot and Guinevere is an allegory, based on much older material, where the Queen is no passive puppet but the Goddess of life and death. Tradition states that the Goddess is loved by the God in his twin personification as the light, creative king and the dark king of the Underworld and decay. These alternate as contenders for Her and remain in balance, as life and death must. This is an esoteric matter, but it lifts the fable of Guinevere on to a different level and leaves us with the Aries desire for what cannot be had.

Forgetting Lancelot as a personification of the Nature god, he is a true Arien figure, and he loves Guinevere not just because she is beautiful and his heart's desire. She is those things, but her main attraction is that she is the Queen and cannot be had. Some Aries waste their lives wanting what cannot be theirs, although the object of desire may vary from time to time. The dynamic behind this is that those Ariens don't really *want* to possess – for that would tie them down, crystallise them, call them to get their hands dirty in the murky water of real relationships. Or the same may apply to the coveted job, the academic accolade. Underneath this there may be a wish to remain 'above it all,' but even deeper there may be a real fear of reality and what might happen if it did all come to pass. Then the dreams would die.

If you recognise yourself in this, perhaps you need to realise that you are wasting your power to imagine – for imagination is supremely creative – on yearning for what can never be. Stop it. Learn to dream possible dreams, and keep them modest. You may still have that big dream in your heart, and maybe it will draw closer. The things you want are a substitute, and you are afraid of failing at what matters most – that certain something that you need to build in life. No Aries is ever held back by fear for long!

## ■ ARIES AND MARRIAGE

Aries tend to take life seriously, and marriage is no exception. Having tied the knot, you will do your best to make it work. You do not need constant physical presence in marriage – in fact, it may be better if one or both partners takes frequent business trips. This is not an excuse and opportunity to 'have a fling'. Aries does stray at times, but rarely thinks it means very much. However, if you find out that your non-Arien partner has been unfaithful, it would be best for him or her to hide! A fair-minded Aries will realise this is a double standard, like having your cake and eating it, and recognise the necessity for compromise. In general Aries does need variety and believes that 'absence makes the heart grow fonder'.

Partners of Ariens must always keep some independence and auton-omy. Aries is a good mate to lean on and enjoys lending a helping hand. You will mop up the tears of a weeping willow, bring flowers, laughter and cheer, but clinging vines are less your style, and you will soon yearn for freedom. Many Aries take a long time to find a suitable marriage partner, for you are fussy and idealistic. If you are an Aries looking for a partner, remember to choose someone who will enter your dreams, and dream a few of her or his own. People who are contemplating marriage with an Aries should make sure that they understand your idealistic side. You may be involved in the most prosaic of jobs but you will always like to feel the door is open to the possible. Of course, physical love is important, but you have a strongly intellectual, abstract streak, and your mind needs stimulat-ing, too. Marriage, as with all else, should provide you with stimulus.

## ■ WHEN LOVE WALKS OUT – HOW ARIES COPES

It happens to all of us at one time or another, and Aries is no exception – the one you love leaves you, usually for someone else. Usually the reaction will be tumultuous and there will be tears and even threats of suicide. Don't underestimate this. Even if it is an idle threat the depth of the emotional trauma is what you want to convey, and it is best that this be appreciated. It really does feel as if the world has ended, for all your dreams have died. The child in us is present to some extent in most of our intimate relationships and when you have given your heart, you are utterly open and vulnerable. 'But I trusted you!' may be the cry. Never mind that you might not always have been totally, utterly trustworthy yourself; that didn't mean anything. Now your world, your dreams and your self-image are shattered in pieces in the dust, and it feels tragic.

This has to take its course. Aries must rage and cry. You do not like to be patronised, minimised or told to 'Snap out of it'. There is a time for sorrow, and it is now, so you want to be left to mourn copiously. Give yourself permission to be broken hearted, have a breakdown, fall to bits. *This won't go on for ever.* Soon you will be able to mythologise even the experience of loss. It's all part of life's rich tapestry after all – and now look, the Sun is shining, a little watery through the rain, but glistening and brightening all the same. Recovery may take a long time if this really was someone special, but there is always another special person, another reason to live and strive, another dream. So grieve, keep faith, and live to love another day. There is no one more lovable, or with more to give than you.

## Starting afresh

This should not happen too soon, for if it does you may launch into something impractical, zany, and even life-threatening in an effort to escape from the pain in your heart. In due time you will need something that you can throw yourself into, that will bring the world back to life. It is better if this is not another relationship just yet. Some other enterprise or adventure will serve better to bring you back on course, so that you will be ready to love again.

As an Aries, your recuperative powers are sure to be strong. Think earnestly about what happened and try to understand it. This is not to find where you went wrong so you can get it right next time – that's not what life and love are about. However, it will help if you are able to see how this experience fits into the fabric of your life and how it has changed you. Be sure to let it change you in some way. If you have grieved fully and let go, you will not be bitter and any change will make you a better person.

---

### ■ PRACTICE AND CHANGE ■

- Remember you need romance in relationships – do not commit yourself to the entirely prosaic.
- Having said this, remember also that men are not gods and women are not goddesses. We all really do have feet of clay – and yes, that does mean even your very own Ms or Mr Wonderful!
- Learn to use your fantasies creatively, to enrich your life. Do not expect anyone to embody them. They are yours, from within you.
- There *is* a boring old 'real world'. If you don't wish it to overwhelm you from time to time, you need to develop a realistic working relationship with it.

This may be a good time to review all your romantic relationships. What have they been like? What have they meant to you? What part have they played in your life? And what do you hope for in the future? We learn so much about ourselves through our choices of partners – or choice of no partners. What have yours taught you, about you?

---

# 3

# All in the family

*My mother groan'd, my father wept,*
*Into the dangerous world I leapt;*
*Helpless, naked, piping loud,*
*Like a fiend hid in a cloud*

William Blake, *Infant Sorrow*

An Aries in the family is not a person who will be ignored. Somehow, somewhere, even the quietest Aries manages to get her or himself noticed and the little ways of the Aries will be well known to their nearest and dearest. Let's take a look at Aries in some of the traditional family roles.

## ■ ARIES MOTHER

It is not unusual for Aries ladies to avoid motherhood altogether, either from conscious choice or unconscious motivation. It is natural for you to wish to explore yourself and your talents to the full. This is, after all, the first sign of the zodiac, corresponding to human consciousness asserting itself in the initial thrill of sensing yourself as a unique, separate entity. It is not easy with this in mind to give yourself over to the nurturing of another, demanding human consciousness. There is that in Aries that wishes to remain an eternal child, and how can you do this and mother someone else?

The answer is that you can, and very well as many Arien mothers demonstrate brilliantly. However, most Aries ladies are keen to build a career for themselves and like to feel that they are bringing home at least half the loaf – and many will efficiently bring home all the bread. You are an independent lady, and the position of motherhood can leave you vulnerable to disappointment. How can you hope to fight your corner, climb to the top of the company hierarchy, write poetry or refine your skills as a concert pianist if you have a child in tow?

Many female Aries do succeed in these things and bring up children at the same time, however, for you have no equal for drive and resourcefulness. The challenge of single parenthood is one that you will rise to, and you won't rush to find a man to help you out. It is rare for Aries to give up her career for motherhood, although some do make a career out of having children. This is only likely to be the case, however, if, as a mother you are spearheading some new movement – Natural Child Care, or Towards a Fresh Psychology of the Young. Then family life will be the laboratory for the experimental approach, zealously applied, and you will evangelise the new methods to all your friends, trying to make as many converts as possible. There is nothing clinical in this, and you are so warm and responsive there need be no fear for the children. They will happily get on with life, playing and growing, unaware that they are embodying any new vision.

The Aries mother is warm-hearted, and fiercely protective. You are unlikely to hesitate to fight for your child if you feel this is necessary. Many a hapless teacher has emerged, shredded, from an encounter with Aries Mum. If a teacher tried to explain that little Ben (probably an Aries as well) has been disrupting the class, an Aries mother would quite likely be of the opinion that if the teacher can't keep control then she shouldn't be in the classroom. You are not slow to discipline your child, however, and you can be firm to the point of ruthlessness on occasion. When you say 'no' you mean no, and your child had better believe it. However, you are always ready with a cuddle and a warm smile, and as your children grow they soon get wise to all the ways to win you over. They learn to appeal to your imagination by discussing some absorbing school project, distract you with tales of how the Big Ones stole their lunch (it was the only way they could get rid of those Marmite sandwiches, which they hate, but which you gave them anyway, because you're health conscious) or just give you a hug. Even motherhood cannot deprive Aries of simplicity.

## ◼ ARIES FATHER

While motherhood brings a sense of realism to the females of the species, the male Arien enters the realm of fatherhood untrammelled and unmodified by biology. Thus you may have many ideas about children in general, and your children in particular, that have little or nothing to do with the little creature placed in your arms – who may well be a Taurus or a Cancer, with a very different world view from yours!

As an Aries dad, you want the very best for your children and will do your utmost to provide it. You would also like them to be the very best at something, preferably of your choosing, but all but the most fanatical Aries are well aware that each human being is an individual. After all, you are a true champion of freedom, and will stand up for the right of your child to choose – almost always. There are some cherished ideals that die hard, however, and if you are an Aries who built up a thriving family business from scratch, you may fight hard to keep your child in the same game when the child is determined to go round the world and 'then see'. However, you can see yourself in the youngster, so after all the fireworks you will settle into a grudging respect for the 'chip off the old block'. In all relationships, you honour those who will stand up for themselves. However, many an Aries dad has a wistful look in his eye as he says something like 'I always wanted a feminine little girl' as his sleek-muscled, adolescent daughter plays ball with the boys out in the street, with her hair flying everywhere! This may seem a sexist example – on a philosophical level Aries dad is not sexist, but sometimes your idealism may seduce you into the pursuit of images that others find constraining.

You are brilliant at playing games and revealing the secret, vibrant core of life to a child. Your store of vivid life experience makes the world an interesting place to grow up in. You may have an irrepressible sense of humour, enjoy sport, be prepared to act out dramas in the living room or read many stories. Aries mum is the same, for these are not boring parents, unless they have been badly bruised and repressed themselves.

There is just a danger with Aries dad that your child may not really be perceived for the special individual she or he actually is. This is possible with Aries mum also, for although she is unlikely to live out her life through her offspring, she may be too busy or too preoccupied really to *see* them, for what they are. It is so important for all Aries parents to remind themselves that there is a here and now, it doesn't matter what you would like it to be or think it might/could be if you try something different – it is how it is and your child is how he or she is. They have come to this Earth for their own purposes, not to fulfil any ideal or preconception that you may have, and your sacred trust is to notice, nurture and affirm their own uniqueness. Your sense of fairness and individuality is sure to respect that – and no one can do it better than you.

## ■ THE ARIES CHILD

An Aries child is certainly a handful – brace yourself! Adolescence is coming, and it isn't likely to get easier – but more of that later. For the moment let us turn to the small Aries. This little character will stamp her mark on the family from the word go. She may well stamp many marks on furniture and wall also, not to mention turning your pet cat into a furry ball of neurosis. Young Aries has the art of food sculpture refined to the fantastic. Is that . . . was that ever a potato? And could that be spaghetti on the lampshade? As for what Aries has in her shell-like ear – best to head for the bathroom and not ask too many questions.

Aries also has clumsiness elevated to a form of ballet. One young Aries boy was engaged in his usual breakfast pastime of relating the plot of the latest sci-fi film in minute detail – each morning it was something similar, or his dreams of the previous night. Leaning one elbow on the table, with the other fist clutching a cereal packet, he described extra-terrestrials and spaceships, shaking cornflakes vigorously in a generally downward direction as he spoke. Having arrived at a suitable point in the plot, he hesitated and looked at his bowl. It was empty. Puzzled, he looked about him, suspecting his elder brother of trickery – but no. The bowl was there, and there was nothing in it, so where were the cornflakes? Had they been beamed up to some spaceship above the house? Moving to investigate, he lowered his propped arm. Out showered the cornflakes, which he had been pouring down his dressing-gown sleeve as he recounted his story. Not many people can achieve a thing like that. The kitchen floor was covered, and Aries' suspicion that the world held some conspiracy to get him was strengthened.

Most children have tantrums, but in this, too, Aries may be extreme. This needs to be treated as firmly and patiently as you can. Stand-up fights with the child should be avoided because often Aries just *can't* back down. Something inside them won't permit it. If you insist on doing such violence to their individuality, then you can't really love them, or so something in Aries says. Aries is fighting that belief as much as you and so she needs to win. If you overcome Aries by sheer force of adult strength, then you will be hurting her deeply, and you may pay for it later when your child is bigger. However, you can't just give in, either. Aries won't respect you and will push you more and more until she dominates the household and all is lost. So what is a poor parent to do? Diplomacy is the answer, and being one jump ahead. Try to avoid scenes of conflict and shower Aries with plenty of attention and affection. If there is no alternative to a stand-off then make sure that you both soon make up afterwards. Sometimes young Aries will make a lunge at you in a sort of aggressive, loving attack, and what she wants is a cuddle. Above all, *always* make it clear that if you reject or condemn anything it is not the child, but only certain behaviour. Grudges should never be held, and if you must punish then do it instantly and let it be over, so warmth can re-establish itself.

When the time comes for school Aries may throw a dreadful tantrum. Why should he leave home and go to that nasty school? However, once Aries realises the scope offered by school his natural confidence will awaken and he will dash into the classroom each morning – head first as usual – eager to see what the day will bring. Aries are usually competitive, and this may be in sport or intellectually. They are usually quick witted also. However, the trouble here may be that it either comes easily or not at all, for little Aries may have scant patience. Although readily rising to a challenge, Aries should not be compared to more able pupils for that may be wounding. They will not be able to bear the fact that someone else is better than them, and they may just not have the werewithall to compete. Humans have different ways of processing information, and Aries may be dyslexic or have some other problem that somehow reflects their intuitive approach to life. Yes, they are very bright, but intelligence is hard to define and takes many shapes. If your Aries thinks differently from other people make sure that he gets the help and appreciation he needs as early as possible in his academic career.

As adolescence approaches and the big, wide world beckons, Aries may seem to retreat to a world of their own at times. Burgeoning sexuality is filling them with all sorts of ideas about themselves and about life, and they will want to play with all of this in their heads. They may fall in love early, but it is more characteristic for Aries to come to this comparatively late. Other exploration may take precedence, and your son or daughter may go on camping trips with friends, or – more worrying – on lone biking expeditions to distant destinations. Some will get lost in books or films, but the spirit of adventure will haunt them in some form. Now your earlier patience and openness will pay off, for adolescent Aries will confide some of her most private thoughts to you, and seek your help. Give your ideas honestly, but don't forget that Aries has to make her own mistakes, and these will be worse if encountered in the shadow of your opposition.

## ■ ARIES AS SIBLINGS

If you have an Aries brother or sister you may be wondering what you have done to deserve it! Older Aries will boss you dreadfully, but there are two consolations. One is that she or he will always champion you if the school bully appears on the horizon. The other is that Aries are usually so bound up in their own dramas that they will, with any luck, leave you alone most of the time. If your Aries sibling is younger he or she will still be bossy, and more both-ersome, for if Aries want help they will demand it, if your music is too loud they will bang on the door until you turn it down (or mum or dad appear) and if you want privacy to be with your friends only some sort of bribe will suffice. If you are a Fire sign yourself you will find much of this par for the course, if not, well, the relationship will improve as you both get older – honestly!

## ■ ARIES IN THE HOME

Aries does not like to be cramped. Some will spread their posses-sions invasively over any available area, taking over the space of others. Some will demand their own special space, where they can be and do what they like. Even if you live in a small house where children have to share rooms, make sure that there is a place that each child, especially young Aries, can call their own. Shared bedrooms should be clearly divided – avoid bunks if you possibly can. Even a different colour carpet to mark out separate space can be a good idea. Younger Aries should have the wall space to display pictures or hang models, and older Aries will wish to put up posters. Adult Aries will need a desk and chair or some such important and individual corner that is their own – and that includes busy and beset Aries mother! Such arrangements will benefit all family members, believe me, not just Aries in question! This may sound territorial, but humans are – and even mice display disturbed behaviour when overcrowded.

Bold colours appeal to Aries, and plenty of room will be needed to store sports equipment, musical instruments, art materials and all the many trappings that Aries needs for a varied life. Aries also often want the window open – some are fanatical about this. The element of Fire seems to manifest literally in that they are often overheated, and a common complaint from young Aries is that they can't sleep because they are too hot – even when their room is about the same temperature as the bottom of the garden, where a lively gale is blowing! Such matters do, of course, depend also on other chart factors, but the strongly Arien temperament becomes overheated when confined. Suppressed rage also will make Aries hot, and so they should be encouraged to express how they feel – gently.

If you have Aries in the house, remember they are sensitive. This is easy to forget when they seem to have been trampling you underfoot all day, but it is so. Try to respect this, and to help them sort out what they really need – for they might not find this easy to articulate – rather than losing your temper. This will make everything smoother for all concerned, for Aries won't – can't – suffer in silence.

---

### ■ PRACTICE AND CHANGE ■

● If you are an Aries parent, remember your children cannot flesh out your dreams, and they have an identity of their own. You can build your own dreams – you owe it to yourself, not only to them.

● Try to avoid confrontations, where possible, with an Aries child. Be one jump ahead. Their determination and stubbornness are a front for vulnerability – try to make sure they don't hurt themselves.

● Encourage your Aries adolescents in their schemes. If you are really in their 'corner' they are more likely to listen to sensible modifications.

● Wherever and however you live, always make sure that Aries family members have their own special space to call their own.

---

# 4 Friendships and the single life

*Better an open enemy than a false friend*

Proverb, seventeenth century

## ■ ARIES AS A FRIEND

If your friend wants you to tell her that her new dress looks great, when the colour doesn't suit her and it makes her look like an army of potatoes fighting inside a bolster case, or a mate who wants you to say that the new tie he bought in a moment of daring isn't going to blind everyone – then they shouldn't ask you, an Aries. You will tell your friends what you think, for you are not good at subtlety and your lies have hobnail boots. Occasionally you will lie, if pushed into a corner, but such falsehoods are usually quite blatant, and as you can't be bothered to remember what you said yesterday you are sure to let yourself down. You are honest – sometimes blisteringly so. However, your friends usually know where they are with you, and while your frankness may hurt them, they may rest assured that they won't have to dodge and parry any of the sneaky darts and innuendoes that pepper some friendships.

They say that a friend in need is a friend indeed, and Aries may well prove to be just that. You are loyal, and when you have decided who are your friends, you will turn up to be at their side at three in the morning, if they need it. You will help them move house when they are leaving their partner – and give them a few home truths given half a chance. You will help them home when they've had a few too many drinks and probably be ready with the 'hair of the dog' the next morning – however, they might have to put up with listening to your advice, uncompromisingly given. Nonetheless, if they take no notice chances are you will be just as ready to help next time – and to repeat the advice. If you trust them, you will lend them most things, from your clothes to your money. You will give them a shoulder to cry on, a bed in the living room, a slap-up meal from the bits and pieces in the fridge, and your opinion – loudly.

While you may be extremely ready with active help and participation, you are not that good at long heart to hearts over endless cups of coffee – unless your friends are talking about your problems, of course, in which case prepare to burn the midnight oil. If they do try to initiate a heart to heart about their own problems they may find that you have decided to go out for a walk while they were in the lavatory. You do not mean to be selfish or nasty but you can be too spontaneous to be able to provide a long outflowing of sympathy – you would rather take your friends out and cheer them up. Amazed, they may see your straight back disappearing down the road, and they may imagine they have mortally offended you. Not so! You got a bit bored and fancied a stroll, and it will never have occurred to you that they might wonder at your sudden departure. You will be back, sooner or later, possibly with a bottle of wine or chocolates under your arm, and a big grin.

Once the friendship is established it has to be said that Aries takes liberties. You will not hesitate to sprawl on the sofa and have a kip if a dinner party is a bit boring. You will choose the CDs and put them on, and you may well not wash up, or deign to notice such an event takes place. It is quite possible that you will turn up to stay with your tribe of noisy kids (surely they can't *all* be Ariens, your friends may wonder?) and not think to tell your friends when you are all going home. More awkwardly, some Ariens are hurt when confronted about this sort of behaviour. You really don't mean to be inconsiderate and you are only behaving that way because you trust them.

You wouldn't mind if they did the same. Aries can take frankness, but only up to a point. Beyond this you may be very hurt, for basically you are warm hearted and innocent.

If your friends value openness, honesty and warmth above tact and diplomacy, if they like to feel sure that what you say to their face is the same as what you say behind their back, if they prize someone who can have a disagreement yet still be cordial and who has the guts to back them when they get into a tight corner, then you are their woman or man – and they are fortunate! If they value you – and I am sure they do – you will be rewarded with responsiveness, tolerance and frankness for you will be respect them for this, but they shouldn't be brutal. You are more sensitive than you appear.

## ■ ARIES AND THE SINGLE LIFE

Many Ariens seem to wind up as loners. This may be because you are often misunderstood or because you find it hard to compromise enough to find a social niche. Often you have a passionate wish to do things that don't seem to appeal to other people, and so you will go your own way. You would much rather have company, but you will go it alone if you have to.

The same applies to long-term partnerships such as marriage. An Aries partner isn't very good at compromise and is reluctant to be tied down. The high-flying career woman is more likely to be an Aries than a Virgo. The single life has its charm for Aries, and Ariens cope with it better than many other signs.

The great gift of being single is independence. You may go to bed when you like and there is no one to object if it's four in the morning (because you were finishing that short story/poem/model of the Starship Enterprise) or it's three in the afternoon, because you feel like it. Holidays may be taken where you wish, there is no one to consult, and who knows who you might meet? And there is no one to make a mess – Aries may not be all that tidy, but you don't like other people's clutter.

If you are Aries and single, make the most of it. You may yearn to have someone to share your life, but ask yourself honestly whether that is because you have been taught to believe you want this, and whether the true benefits of being single are more valuable to you. Being single gives you time and opportunity to do and be what you want, and it gives you lots of space to cultivate friendships.

Aries is rarely a clingy sign, and often you are quite incapable of compromising your individuality for the sake of friendships or relationships. It's not that you don't want – and need – companions and closeness. Rather it is that you just don't really know how to compromise. When you try, you may be clumsy and abrupt, and friends may feel you are trying to force compromise upon them! You do need to cultivate a vivid awareness of your manner, if you wish more friendships to blossom. You may need to remind yourself to be gentle and take a deep breath or two while your companion responds – and *really* listen.

Some Ariens do not quite see other people as real personalities, but rather as players in life's drama – two dimensional figures that form the backdrop of life but have no full identity of their own. This may be because you are so preoccupied with your own self-expression that you do not have room to encompass the real presence of others. If you are in the habit of perceiving people thus, it can be hard to become aware of it. Of course, it is probably not your role in life to be always taking into account the preferences of others. However, you will achieve more if you get into the habit of at least remembering that others may feel and react very differently from you. As an Aries you are a leader, and sometimes you will stride off alone on your projects – but it is so much nicer when someone follows!

## ■ PRACTICE AND CHANGE ■

● When your foot strays into your mouth, try to be a little aware of how your words and actions are affecting others. Other people can be deeply hurt, even though you might not mean it.

● Just because someone really likes you or is a member of your family, doesn't mean that you can have *carte blanche* to do what you like in their house, with their things. Of course, you mean no harm and if you do this people do realise – for the most part – that you're only acting that way because you feel secure and at home, but . . . would *you* be able to put up with it?

● If you are on your own and telling yourself you don't want to be, ask yourself whether this is really the case, or if you are merely conditioned not to like it? Being with someone else requires a lot of compromise. Are you prepared?

Perhaps you have decided that you are not satisfied with life as it is and you would like more friends. In this, as in all things, you will need to be proactive. To make new friends you have to go out and be where other people may be who also want new friends. It isn't enough just to go out and be friendly. There are people whose social life is full and, although they may like you, they won't have time or room for you. Often the lonely people stay at home, feeling forlorn. If you are true to your sign you will not want to be one of them. Keep searching until you find companions, do not be hurt or put off if you have failures and feel you have been brushed off. Do not waste time on those who obviously are already busy. Your zest and enthusiasm is just what someone is wanting in his or her life!

# 5 Career

*Nothing great was ever achieved without enthusiasm*

Ralph Waldo Emerson

Aries is a pioneer, and nowhere is this more in evidence than in their profession. You like to blaze a trail, and you crave recognition, often the more public the better. Intensely ambitious, you aim straight for the top.

Of course, as we have often said, there are quieter Aries. Some of you have been crushed in some way, but deep in your hearts you will never give up – hope springs eternal in the Aries breast. You secretly imagine the big break, the great and wonderful chance will be yours some day, and all of life will be altered. Other Ariens are quiet, not because you have been repressed but rather it is your natural mode. What you seek is more abstract and internal, the flames of the spirit, the silent glory of the inner breakthrough, but almost without exception you are playing for important stakes, and you want to make changes and leave your mark.

## ■ TRADITIONAL ARIES CAREERS

The common denominator for all occupations suitable for Ariens is that they involve some degree of cut and thrust, either literal or metaphoric. Aries careers include:

- soldier
- engineer
- foundry or metal worker
- fire fighter

- sportsperson
- dentist
- surgeon
- mechanic
- explorer
- butcher

- engine driver
- arms manufacturer
- sword maker
- trade unionist
- psychiatrist
- psychologist

# ■ WHAT TO LOOK FOR IN YOUR WORK

As we all know, it can be very difficult to find a fulfilling career. To help you find a job that suits you, you need to bear in mind the *spirit* of the career, not the specific occupation. Also think about the particular details of any job. One office job is not like another, one shop selling fashions may differ enormously from one down the street in terms of environment and opportunity. Aries needs to keep a keen eye on the general approach of an organisation when you go for interview and make sure of several things when seeking employment:

- There is scope for advancement.
- The company or person you work for is going to welcome initiative and value your personal input.
- There is something that is going to stimulate you on a day-to-day level.
- A certain flexibility about time is not going to send your employer into orbit. This doesn't mean you can be a layabout and have every Friday off. Nor does it mean you can possibly come in late when you have to open the shop at 9 a.m. However, when it is possible there should be a degree of flexibility. If you are interested in your job you may well choose to work late, but you are going to feel discouraged if someone is clock watching when you are five minutes late back from lunch.

- You are not tied to rigid routine, doing the same thing day after day, hour after hour.
- Most Aries do like to be mobile in their work. Unless the job is very mentally stimulating, and that is your bent, you will need to move around physically, meet new people, encounter new ideas.

Despite these pointers, do remember there is no need to feel that you have to look for a specifically Arien job. Many Aries would be bored to death by metal working and ideologically opposed to arms manufacture. Look for something that suits in its content and atmosphere, rather than its label. If it doesn't suit, move on.

## ■ THE LAZY RAM

We have seen that Aries can be lazy on occasion, and naturally this trait will be the enemy of successful employment. Aries become lazy for several reasons. One of these is that you secretly feel inadequate, but won't admit to it. Then you may take refuge in saying you can't be bothered. Nothing can ship you into life's backwaters quicker than that attitude, and you will hate that. Face up what you can't do – who said you had to be perfect? Maybe with some – dare I say it? – help, you can sort out that problem and progress. If not, you have to move elsewhere, to what you can do, as soon as possible.

Another background to laziness may be disdain. Many Aries – if not all – have lofty ideas, and when these do not seem to materialise you may escape from a sense of failure into looking down your nose at the demeaning occupation life has somehow betrayed you into. It is true that some are luckier than others, but it is also true that you make your own luck. If you can do better then you must prove this, and if not, be the best you can at what you've got.

# ■ THE OFFICE TYRANT

This character is one of the most negative sides of Aries. Here is a Ram that missed the mark and got shunted into a siding. The office tyrant doesn't like petty paper-pushing, doesn't like being stuck behind a desk while all the fresh-faced youngsters ride off in their company cars. This Aries will use all the meagre authority of many years with the company to make colleagues' lives a misery, because he or she is miserable. The anger and frustration are enough to corrode the filing cabinets and give a virus to the computer.

All others can do is pity this character – 'he' is usually male, although the female version is occasionally found. There is nothing for him to look forward to, because that gold watch will only remind him of his failed ambitions. And if – saddest of all – you spot yourself in this description, then get out! Believe me, even the disruption and upheaval of change is better than soul-destroying routine.

# ■ THE ARIES BOSS

This person will expect a great deal. He or she is generally dynamic and committed 101 per cent, and will expect the same of others. The Aries boss may ball out subordinates in front of their colleagues, but he or she will also be prepared to hear their side of the story – which must be put firmly and clearly. Aries usually says what he or she means, and subordinates needn't fear too much that a file on their misdemeanours is lurking and growing in the managerial desk.

If you are an Aries boss you probably will encourage new talent. If you have made it this far you're not going to be afraid of competition, and many Aries are too ingenuous and far too straight even to think of appropriating other people's ideas as their own. You will appreciate others for offering you greater stimulus and challenge. In any case, you probably have lots of good ideas of your own. You won't expect colleagues to stick to the rules, but their respect for hierarchy will be required – all the Fire signs have a sense of the pecking order and usually strive to ensure that they are well placed in it.

No doubt you are a creative person whose life experience and inner life are very varied. You won't nurse subordinates along but you can be most caring. This is especially so for female Ariens, who will often be warm and encouraging to those below them on the ladder. Aries really needs and appreciates loyalty and support, especially when the going gets tough. If colleagues don't let you down, they will have someone who will be their eternal champion.

## ■ THE ARIES EMPLOYEE

It will be evident from the first interview for a job that the Aries employee is a person who has a reasonably high opinion of themselves. Some potential employers find this threatening, and it is doubtful whether a Capricorn or Taurus would be impressed. However, open-minded bosses will find enthusiastic Aries irresistible.

You have probably found out all about the company and have come armed with some fresh, if naive suggestions for improving it. You will be all fired up about what you have to offer the company and what it has to offer you. If an employer decides to employ an Aries they should let you have your head as much as possible. If they don't breathe down your neck, but make it clear that they expect results, the chances are their expectations will be more than rewarded. They shouldn't expect Aries always to be in on time, either, and if this really doesn't matter, they shouldn't be pedantic about it, for if Aries' interest is aroused, he or she will be doing more than the fair share. As for money, Aries is alive to the potential money brings to open pathways to new experience. However, money isn't likely to be the prime motive for any Aries taking on a job. Fulfilment is a far higher priority. Give Aries a piece of the action, scope for promotion and place reliance on them when under pressure. The chances are Aries will justify an employer's faith.

## ■ WHEN UNEMPLOYMENT STRIKES

We all know this does happen. Sometimes it is a surprise and sometimes you can prepare for it. Mostly it has nothing to do with your ability and has everything to do with company reorganisation and cut-backs. However, unemployment hits Aries just where it hurts – in your pride.

The main things to remember in this situation are: don't try to pretend you don't feel hurt, least of all to yourself; don't stand still (although you are allowed one night of drowning your sorrows) – get on and apply for new jobs immediately; try to regard this as an opportunity to explore new avenues. As long as you keep a positive attitude you will be fine. Remember that work doesn't have the monopoly on significance in your life. Maybe now you have some time for other creative pastimes. However, don't soar so high from the mundane that you forget the mortgage has to be paid!

## ■ SELF-EMPLOYMENT AND OTHER MATTERS

Not all work relies on a company and an employer, for there are many other approaches. Aries is intensely creative and inventive and you may well start up a business of your own or work freelance in the arts or publishing. In fact, Aries is supremely suited to any manner of enterprise that needs independence and talent. Aries may be poets or sculptors, performers or writers, for each of these occupations pushes back known boundaries in its own way. If you are contemplating going it alone, my advice is to make sure you have sound financial management.

---

### ■ PRACTICE AND CHANGE ■

- Make sure that any job you choose has scope for advancement, room for movement and stimulus.
- If you get frustrated, try to make sure this doesn't render you immobile with resentment – convert all energies to activity.
- Make sure your job offers a challenge.
- Ensure there is room for your creativity.
- Do not commit yourself to a routine you will find crushing.

This could be a good moment to list all your talents and all the things you like to do, from the grandest down to the most mundane. These are all part of the portfolio of what you have to offer. You could also list the roles you play in life – partner, sister, brother, parent, son, daughter, boss, employee – the one who cheers everyone up, the ideas person, the one who organises outings, etc. Add to the list as days go by and you think of new things. What do you enjoy most? What could be developed better? Perhaps there is something that you do routinely and take for granted that signifies some unique talent. Make it your mission to be the best Aries, the best person you can be, and see where that leads you.

---

# 6 Healthy, wealthy – and wise?

*A fool and his money are soon parted*

*Health is better than wealth*

Traditional proverbs

## ■ HEALTH

Astrological reflections on health, even when based on the entire birth chart, may be of doubtful value or accuracy because astrology translates better into the psychological rather than the physical. What may we usefully say about the health of Ariens in general?

The Mars energy is usually strong in Aries and because of this you may push yourself to the limit, not noticing you are tired until you are exhausted. This may be especially true for children, who will need to be watched so that they don't work themselves up into that strange state of being 'too tired to sleep'. Aries may be prone to aching joints and muscles from overdoing it.

Because Aries are not terribly well connected to their bodies, all sorts of conditions may develop unnoticed in the early stages, and you may be prostrate before you know you are ill. You need to remind yourself at all times to adopt sensible habits, to eat regularly and well and to take moderate exercise. This may sound obvious, but to many Aries – especially Arien males – it is all too easily neglected.

There is a rather different kind of Aries who is more aware of the body but mistrusts it. Because the element of Fire is the most rarefied and insubstantial, Aries people often do not feel part of the material world. Your body may seem to you an unreliable contraption, inadequate to the purposes you set and liable to let you down unexpectedly. This suspicion of the body can turn many a Fire sign individual into a health freak, always trying the latest macrobiotic/ high vitamin/high energy/fat free/vegan diet. In this way you are looking for the best, the exceptional, the way to make the body in some way larger than life, invincible and able to transcend the confines of flesh. Or you may simply be looking for a way to health, but are somehow unable to approach this in an ordinary way.

In addition, many Aries will try a variety of therapies for ailments that are often hard to define. Looking for optimum vigour and longevity, everything is sampled – acupuncture, aromatherapy, allergy testing, hypnotherapy, homoeopathy . . . the list goes on. Each of these approaches has value in itself, but you may expect too much too quickly and find satisfaction nowhere. If you have found a good, well-qualified therapist who is trying to help you, stick with it. There isn't any magic answer, but there may be slow improvement in whatever is bothering you.

## Headaches, fever and accidents

Aries rules the head and Aries people do seem to have a tendency to more headaches than average, probably because you become angry and overwrought and this produces the tension that causes headaches. Pent-up anger can cause migraines. In *You Can Heal Your Life*, Louise Hay states that headaches may be due to an invalidation of the self, and self-criticism. This may not sound like a typical Arien problem, and yet many Aries people do not come up to the high standards they set themselves, and so give themselves a hard time. Aries can treat life as though it has to be a fight of some description, and that may not be at all 'self-validating; but may mean one wastes a great deal of energy at times, proving points that are not important. Feverfew leaves eaten regularly are said to reduce migraine, and lavender oil placed on the forehead is often soothing.

Many Mars people find that when they have an infection they run a high temperature, but that they soon recuperate. This is more likely to be true if the planet Mars is also strongly placed in the horoscope. In general it is better to let a fever take its course, for the fever is doing its job of protecting the body, and if removed by aspirin or some such, illness may be more prolonged. As always, in any situation which is worrying, qualified help should be sought.

If you watch Aries children playing you may well spot that they often fall and bang themselves, and while they may be too preoccupied to complain, Aries children usually have more than their fair share of bumps and bruises – especially to the head! One Aries boy – in the interests of science, you understand – experimented with throwing a stone exactly vertically. The stone was the largest one he could manage to fling and it came straight down – as Newton had observed they do – and hit him right on the head. Bullseye! Only an Aries child could manage that! A trip to hospital and five stitches followed.

Another Arien little boy managed to split his skull at the front one day and at the back the day after. It is a great embarrassment to arrive at a hospital emergency department with your child's head covered in blood, to be asked whether he has ever been to hospital before and to be forced to reply 'Yes, yesterday'. Three stitches in the front and five at the back, and from the howling you'd think he was being murdered! However, Aries do not always learn their lessons, for the same child, on returning home, launched himself off the bannister and was only saved from another – and far worse – injury by the fact his father was able to catch him. Never mind. Later in the year he managed to knock out one of his teeth, while tilting his stool at the meal table, and to follow it up with a whole range of blood-curdling injuries to the face as he learnt to ride a bike. Never a dull moment with an Aries child!

# ■ MONEY

It cannot really be said that the typical Aries is very good with money. Some Aries spend their money fast and furiously. It burns a hole in their pocket. What's the point of keeping it? Let's live for today – what does it matter? There will always be more around the corner. Other Aries are genuinely unaware of money. They don't know what they've got in the bank and an investigation into pockets and purses may turn up a sheaf of notes or a meagre coin or two. Such Ariens are reasonably happy. Money doesn't bother them too much and somehow they always get by. They have faith in life – and perhaps a money-conscious partner, paying bills and arranging insurance.

However, you may be the other type of Aries who struggles with money and tries to be realistic but somehow never manages to cut your coat according to your cloth. You may work out expenditure, but something always gets forgotten, or you couldn't resist that leather coat/exotic holiday/state-of-the-art exercise machine. Or possibly you are an Aries who hasn't quite come to grips with the world and found your niche in employment. In such a case, money is an eternal bedevilment. We all have financial concerns, but what to Taurus or Capricorn is a necessary task can turn into every Arien's *bête noire*, and they may develop a terror of bank statements and bills.

If this is you, you have several choices. You can turn your finances over to someone else whom you know has good credentials – chances are you won't like that alternative. Or you can make a massive attempt to get it sorted, once and for all, to make a list of all your outgoings and *be realistic* – a necessary stage in this is to make the transition from enjoying spending to enjoying being in control. Or a third alternative may be to make some drastic changes in lifestyle. Work in the evenings and at weekends – you will get more money and have less time to spend it. Decide you will go abroad to work. Apply for better-paid jobs that you have always told yourself you won't get. After all, you never know! Where is that Arien cheek?

## ■ WISDOM

We all know that wisdom is something that transcends health and wealth, and many of us take a lifetime (and some say many lifetimes) to acquire it. Every Aries knows quite well, deep inside, that true wisdom is about the eternal and the inexpressible. It is part of your life quest to pursue your own form of it.

As an Aries, your brand of wisdom is unlikely to be of the quiet, passive mode, but rather about pushing back the boundaries of consciousness, about exploration – either physically or mentally – and the acquisition of wider perspectives. You should never allow yourself to be confined, conceptually, for that could make you short-tempered and intolerant.

Culturally, we are rather wedded to finding 'The Truth' rather than a truth that is valid for us. As an Aries the quest itself, the journey, is more important than arrival. Try to let go of the need to feel you have achieved the ultimate – that you have 'cracked it'. Always be open to new questions, and new awareness of exploration. Aries needs this sort of internal challenge, or they do seem to 'eat their heart out'. In this respect, Aries men may need more scope, and may tend more to the abstract than Aries women, for women will often prove more pragmatic and willing to work with what is at hand. However, for all Aries, your way to wisdom, however you may define it, is through exploration of some kind.

## ■ PRACTICE AND CHANGE ■

**Health**

- Try to resist the urge to follow 'fads'.
- Remember that it is a medical fact that there is no such thing as a physically perfect adult body, so do not waste your time in search of it. The same also goes for the mind.
- Plan a sensible routine that takes the minimum of time, so you won't become impatient with it. Make sure health basics – rest, nutrition and exercise – are covered.
- You may tend to worry unnecessarily about your health. Seek medical advice immediately or put it out of your mind.

**Wealth**

- Arrange your finances so you can't spend everything – a standing order to a Unit Trust account, for instance.
- Cut your coat according to your cloth. Obvious? Yes, but so many Aries manage to ignore it! The plain truth is you will be more free and more in control if you can find a way to get a kick out of managing money, rather than spending it.
- Don't be afraid of a radical change of lifestyle if there really is too much month left and the end of the money!

Anyone – and Aries is no exception – can benefit from a sensible, non-fanatical diet, and most people like their finances well organised. However, it is up to you. How much time do you want to spend on these things? Perhaps it really doesn't matter to you. Perhaps the fussy details of life just stifle you. Well that's fine. You may need to give yourself permission to be what you are instead of going about doing what society seems to expect of you, and seething deep inside. Beyond a few basics you may wish to ignore practicalities – and why not? How boring if we were all housekeepers!

# 7 ♈ Style and leisure

> ... *While the young lambs bound*
> *As to the tabor's sound*

Wordsworth, *Ode on Intimations of Immortality*

## ■ YOUR LEISURE

As an Aries, you probably work hard, and so you need to play hard. It is often said that Aries likes sport. This is by no means always the case, although there does seem to be that within the sign that seems to thrive on competition. However, Aries may often engage in sport or keep fit to prove you can knock your body into shape and overcome the limits of flesh – you do not always do it for the sheer enjoyment.

If you are a typical Aries it may be quite hard for you to 'let go' and enjoy yourself, for you are always trying so hard, in some way, to achieve something. Whatever you choose to do with your leisure, it will need to be something absorbing, preferably that takes you over, mind and body, and leaves you feeling in some way renewed at the end. The child in Aries does need to play, because only by doing this can you experience that intensity of self to which you aspire. When children play, we know quite well that this is no idle amusement – if there is such a thing – but a necessary process in learning about life and their own abilities. Play is equally necessary for adults. When we are 'playing' we are in a state of free association, where many things may enter our minds that the tension of ordinary life normally precludes.

As an Aries, you need to remember that play will refresh you and give you renewed energy. You also need to realise that some of your best ideas will come to you when you are relaxed, so do try not to frown and grit your teeth, but find something to do where mind and body flow.

Competitive sports such as squash, badminton, tennis or even boxing certainly help to bring out the Mars energies, and they can be useful also for making friends. Aries may like to try some of the martial arts – and this can apply especially to Aries ladies. Team sports are not always so good, for although you will love it when everyone is patting you on the back because you've scored a hat-trick, you won't take so kindly to shouts of 'Pass it here' or to insults. You might also like to consider jogging or cross-country running, for these can be very free-ing to the mind. If you must turn it into a competition, set a stop watch to try to beat your own record, but while you are running, do let your mind range far and wide as your heart beats quickly.

Aries of the very self-absorbed type often turn self-exploration into a type of hobby, and may try a variety of therapists and counsellors, thus using up a lot of spare cash and time. This sounds like a very adult pursuit, but do bear in mind that you may be seeking to become a little boy or a little girl again. Most of us do this to some extent, but it may become a preoccupation with Aries, in particular. Naturally, a good therapist will pick this up, but in the end the only person who can pull you up by your bootstraps is you.

More introverted Aries may escape into films or plays, but generally they will need to *do* something with what they have experienced. If they have seen a good film then they will want to tell someone about it. Aries are not content to sink into a quiet doze. As an Aries, you will become very irritable if you expect yourself to remain sedentary and passive for too long. Also you should always seek to do something with what you have absorbed.

Many Aries have dramatic talent, so the local dramatic society might welcome new blood. Have you thought of metal working, carving objects in wood, horse riding or rally driving? Noisy, lively pursuits aren't every Aries' cup of tea, but you certainly need creative outlets, and may be able to write imaginative poetry, play music or sculpt. If you have never tried anything like this – or tried and been told you were useless – try again. You may have an individual, rather whacky style, which may not have been appreciated by teachers and parents, and this may need a chance to grow. In short, if you enjoy something, do it. Vincent Van Gogh was an Aries (see his birth chart on page 5). He lived a life of poverty and rejection, treated like an old dog in his own home, and no one understood or valued his work. His visions and paintings were slightly ahead of their times, yet now they are regarded as brilliant and seminal. Have the courage of your convictions – who is to say that what you do is not wonderful, or going to be worth a fortune one day?

## Holidays

When you plan your holiday, don't be persuaded by friends or family members to take a package holiday or one that offers only a lazy time and a lot of sitting around. For the first few days of your holiday you will need time to unwind – and this is prime time for migraines, that seem to affect those who have maintained tension for a long time, at just the point when they relax.

However, as your holiday progresses you must have stimulation, change and plenty to interest you. What exactly this may be depends on you. If you are of a physical bent then naturally sport such as climbing, hang gliding, wind surfing or abseiling may be good to try. If you are more artistic or intellectual, then choose something like a holiday that incorporates your activity – for instance, a painting and sketching course on a rugged coastline. A really adventurous holiday such as a safari, or something demanding like pony-trekking suits lots of those with Aries in the chart. If you can afford it, holidays to the most out-of-the-way, exotic and unusual places are great for Aries – for example, Outer Mongolia, or Antarctica (or the Moon, as soon as technology offers it!).

## ■ YOUR STYLE

As an Aries your style is generally one of freedom, dash and brightness. You don't like to be confined by your clothes or your lifestyle. Casual clothes suit you best and female Ariens like to wear trousers a lot, for they allow for more movement. The current trend for informal gear and sporty clothes suits Aries fine, but you will also like to look dramatic sometimes, and will need the occasional formal or striking outfit. Colours should be bright or definite – nothing fussy or floaty. Your hairstyle should be easy to maintain, and many female Aries like short hair. As an Aries you may worry a lot about your hair, which never seems 'quite right', so it is worth investing in a good cut.

Your living space needs to be spacious – you don't like to have to fiddle about tidying and sorting, although disorder will get you down, also, for you will feel held back by it. As many mod cons as possible suit your impatient approach – you want to do something more interesting than stir the scrambled egg. Clean lines, light, strong colours and some unusual artefacts will suit your nature best. You also like to feel you have the tools for whatever job may present itself, so a place for these will be needed, sorted, clean and ready for action.

When you are choosing purchases for yourself or your home, think:

- action
- clarity
- smooth movement
- simplicity
- vivid
- useful
- modern
- fast
- free
- stimulating

## ■ PRACTICE AND CHANGE ■

Often you will buy on impulse, and that's no bad thing, but make sure the shop will accept a return, and keep your receipt! Aries are impatient shoppers but living with mistakes will rankle.

- Remember that freedom of movement, clear lines, simplicity and impact are your hallmark.
- You need to 'play hard' so find something absorbing.
- You like a challenge, even in leisure.
- You may have talents that are unsuspected – give it a go!
- You must have some adventure in your life.

Open your wardrobe and take a good look at what's inside. Firstly, do you have anything red? For Aries red is a good colour, for it matches your fiery nature. If your wardrobe is full of pastels, beiges and greys is that really what you want, or have you been pressurised into buying? Naturally the rest of your chart, especially your Moon, Venus, Rising Sign and Midheaven will have lots of bearing on your taste and image.

What about usefulness and comfort? Anything not worn for a year can safely be discarded. Make room right now for some new ideas and new clothes, based on what you have learnt about yourself in these pages. Of course, not everything you have read will apply, but anything that strikes a chord should be taken into consideration. You may not be able to afford a large outlay, but forming an image, deciding on a look that expresses the real you is part of the battle. The way you feel inside determines how you look, but it is also true that your appearance will change the way you feel. What 'me' would you like to be? Decide that you will buy and wear only things that express this, from now on. This can have subtle but far-reaching effects.

# Appendix 1

## ■ ARIES COMBINED WITH MOON SIGN

Our 'birth sign' or 'star sign' refers to the sign of the zodiac occupied by the Sun when we were born. This is also called our 'Sun sign' and this book is concerned with Aries as a Sun sign. However, as we saw in the Introduction, a horoscope means much more than the position of the Sun alone. All the other planets have to be taken into consideration by an astrologer. Of great importance is the position of the Moon.

The Moon completes a tour of the zodiac in about twenty-eight days, changing sign every two days or so. The Moon relates to our instincts, responses, reactions, habits, comfort zone and 'where we live' emotionally – and sometimes physically. It is very important in respect of our intuitional abilities and our capacity to feel part of our environment, but because what the Moon rules is usually non-verbal and non-rational, it has been neglected. This has meant that our lives have become lop-sided. Learning to be friends with our instincts can lead to greater well-being and wholeness.

Consult the table on page 80 to find which sign the Moon was in at the time of your birth. This, combined with your Sun sign is a valuable clue to deeper understanding.

# Find your Moon number

Look up your month and day of birth. Then read across to find your
personal Moon number. Now go to Chart 2, below.

| January | | February | | March | | April | | May | | June | |
|---|---|---|---|---|---|---|---|---|---|---|---|
| 1,2 | 1 | 1,2 | 3 | 1,2 | 3 | 1,2 | 5 | 1,2 | 6 | 1,2 | 8 |
| 3,4 | 2 | 3,4 | 4 | 3,4 | 4 | 3,4 | 6 | 3,4 | 7 | 3,4 | 9 |
| 5,6 | 3 | 5,6 | 5 | 5,6 | 5 | 5,6 | 7 | 5,6 | 8 | 5,6,7 | 10 |
| 7,8 | 4 | 7,8 | 6 | 7,8 | 6 | 7,8 | 8 | 7,8 | 9 | 8,9 | 11 |
| 9,10 | 5 | 9,10,11 | 7 | 9,10 | 7 | 9,10,11 | 9 | 9,10 | 10 | 10,11,12 | 12 |
| 11,12 | 6 | 12,13 | 8 | 11,12 | 8 | 12,13 | 10 | 11,12,13 | 11 | 13,14 | 1 |
| 13,14 | 7 | 14,15 | 9 | 13,14 | 9 | 14,15,16 | 11 | 14,15,16 | 12 | 15,16,17 | 2 |
| 15,16,17 | 8 | 16,17,18 | 10 | 15,16,17 | 10 | 17,18 | 12 | 17,18 | 1 | 18,19 | 3 |
| 18,19 | 9 | 19,20 | 11 | 18,19 | 11 | 19,20,21 | 1 | 19,20 | 2 | 20,21 | 4 |
| 20,21 | 10 | 21,22,23 | 12 | 20,21,22 | 12 | 22,23 | 2 | 21,22,23 | 3 | 22,23 | 5 |
| 22,23,24 | 11 | 24,25 | 1 | 23,24,25 | 1 | 24,25 | 3 | 24,25 | 4 | 24,25 | 6 |
| 25,26 | 12 | 26,27,28 | 2 | 26,27 | 2 | 26,27,28 | 4 | 26,27 | 5 | 26,27 | 7 |
| 27,28,29 | 1 | 29 | 3 | 28,29 | 3 | 29,30 | 5 | 28,29 | 6 | 28,29,30 | 8 |
| 30,31 | 2 | | | 30,31 | 4 | | | 30,31 | 7 | | |

| July | | August | | September | | October | | November | | December | |
|---|---|---|---|---|---|---|---|---|---|---|---|
| 1,2 | 9 | 1 | 10 | 1,2 | 12 | 1,2 | 1 | 1,2,3 | 3 | 1,2 | 4 |
| 3,4 | 10 | 2,3 | 11 | 3,4 | 1 | 3,4 | 2 | 4,5 | 4 | 3,4 | 5 |
| 5,6,7 | 11 | 4,5,6 | 12 | 5,6,7 | 2 | 5,6 | 3 | 6,7 | 5 | 5,6 | 6 |
| 8,9 | 12 | 7,8 | 1 | 8,9 | 3 | 7,8,9 | 4 | 8,9 | 6 | 7,8,9 | 7 |
| 10,11,12 | 1 | 9,10 | 2 | 10,11 | 4 | 10,11 | 5 | 10,11 | 7 | 10,11 | 8 |
| 13,14 | 2 | 11,12,13 | 3 | 12,13 | 5 | 12,13 | 6 | 12,13 | 8 | 12,13 | 9 |
| 15,16 | 3 | 14,15 | 4 | 14,15 | 6 | 14,15 | 7 | 14,15 | 9 | 14,15 | 10 |
| 17,18 | 4 | 16,17 | 5 | 16,17 | 7 | 16,17 | 8 | 16,17,18 | 10 | 16,17 | 11 |
| 19,20 | 5 | 18,19 | 6 | 18,19 | 8 | 18,19 | 9 | 19,20 | 11 | 18,19,20 | 12 |
| 21,22,23 | 6 | 20,21 | 7 | 20,21,22 | 9 | 20,21 | 10 | 21,22,23 | 12 | 21,22 | 1 |
| 24,25 | 7 | 22,23 | 8 | 23,24 | 10 | 22,23,24 | 11 | 24,25 | 1 | 23,24,25 | 2 |
| 26,27 | 8 | 24,25 | 9 | 25,26,27 | 11 | 25,26 | 12 | 26,27,28 | 2 | 26,27 | 3 |
| 28,29 | 9 | 26,27,28 | 10 | 28,29 | 12 | 27,28,29 | 1 | 29,30 | 3 | 28,29 | 4 |
| 30,31 | 10 | 29,30 | 11 | 30 | 1 | 30,31 | 2 | | | 30,31 | 5 |
| | | 31 | 12 | | | | | | | | |

# Find your Moon sign

Find your year of birth. Then read across to the column of your Moon number.
Where they intersect shows your Moon sign.

| Birth year | | | | | Moon number |
|---|---|---|---|---|---|
| | | | | | 1  2  3  4  5  6  7  8  9  10  11  12 |
| 1900 | 1919 | 1938 | 1957 | 1976 | (zodiac symbols) |
| 1901 | 1920 | 1939 | 1958 | 1977 | (zodiac symbols) |
| 1902 | 1921 | 1940 | 1959 | 1978 | (zodiac symbols) |
| 1903 | 1922 | 1941 | 1960 | 1979 | (zodiac symbols) |
| 1904 | 1923 | 1942 | 1961 | 1980 | (zodiac symbols) |
| 1905 | 1924 | 1943 | 1962 | 1981 | (zodiac symbols) |
| 1906 | 1925 | 1944 | 1963 | 1982 | (zodiac symbols) |
| 1907 | 1926 | 1945 | 1964 | 1983 | (zodiac symbols) |
| 1908 | 1927 | 1946 | 1965 | 1984 | (zodiac symbols) |
| 1909 | 1928 | 1947 | 1966 | 1985 | (zodiac symbols) |
| 1910 | 1929 | 1948 | 1967 | 1986 | (zodiac symbols) |
| 1911 | 1930 | 1949 | 1968 | 1987 | (zodiac symbols) |
| 1912 | 1931 | 1950 | 1969 | 1988 | (zodiac symbols) |
| 1913 | 1932 | 1951 | 1970 | 1989 | (zodiac symbols) |
| 1914 | 1933 | 1952 | 1971 | 1990 | (zodiac symbols) |
| 1915 | 1934 | 1953 | 1972 | 1991 | (zodiac symbols) |
| 1916 | 1935 | 1954 | 1973 | 1992 | (zodiac symbols) |
| 1917 | 1936 | 1955 | 1974 | 1993 | (zodiac symbols) |
| 1918 | 1937 | 1956 | 1975 | 1994 | (zodiac symbols) |

Legend: Ari  Tau  Gem  Can  Leo  Vir  Lib  Sco  Sag  Cap  Aqu  Pis

## Aries Sun / Aries Moon

You are the true zodiacal *enfant terrible.* Your energy and enthusiasm are almost boundless, and you throw all of yourself and more into most things you attempt. You may be especially prone to lose your temper, but you soon recover. Extremely impatient, you do need to beware that you are not provoked to violence at times, for although this may be purely verbal, others may still be reeling after you have forgotten the incident and moved on to something else. Tact is most unlikely to be your strong point but you can be sensitive, and many people would be surprised at how deeply hurt you can be deep down. Temporarily you may feel quite crushed. You may need to learn to distinguish your real needs from the voice that clamours 'I want', for only in this way can you nurture yourself and find your true individuality.

## Aries Sun / Taurus Moon

This is a most fertile combination, for you possess both the ability to envision new ways and to put them into practice. You can be very efficient and may accomplish a surprising amount because you do not waste energy. You may be conscious of an inner frustration because your need for security and stability gets in the way of your dynamism, and you may rarely feel quite content. Possibly you may invest a lot of your energy in feathering your nest, and wonder why you never feel really safe. Take the time to walk in the country or in some other way relax close to nature, to make contact with what you truly need. Your Arien nature will be freed if you are able to let go of what gives you no true nurture – for example, too much food, material things, sex, lazy or clingy habits – and in turn your energies can move to make you truly secure, in a way that fulfils your soul and enables you to give and create.

## Aries Sun / Gemini Moon

You are quite a restless person and people may tell you that you have ants in your pants! You are able to find many ways to get what you want – you are rarely beaten or down for long! It may be quite hard for you to know how you are really feeling and you may escape from emotions into action. You love energetic interaction, but this may remain superficial – often you do not like to be too serious. It may be hard for you to make commitments, but then your life may lack the intensity craved by Aries. You are probably quite clever and you need to use your mind to think about your needs and relationships, instead of escaping from them into restless activity or abstract thought. In this way you may find a place both of rest and stimulation.

## Aries Sun / Cancer Moon

This is not the easiest combination, but it has tremendous potential. Often you will feel pulled two ways, drawn into situations where your compassion is aroused, and most frustrated that you can't seem to do anything about it. Sensitive to the pain of others, you may often go rather insensitively about helping them! You may also be impatient of your own inner wounds – we all have them – and may seek to escape from the effects of childhood unhappiness by strenuously engaging in anything and everything. Then you may find your path eternally crossed by clinging, needy people. You may not be aware of how demanding you are in relationships. Learn to be kind to your own child within and recognise your vulnerability, for you may be confusing the needs of others with your own – it may be necessary to keep them needy rather than face your own neediness. But it is wounds that make us human and lovable, and your initiative can only move to heal them once they have been identified.

## Aries Sun / Leo Moon

You are a sunny person and you feel instinctively confident that you can accomplish all that you wish. You do rather like to be the boss but people often forgive you, for you take charge so innocently and enthusiastically – and mostly you do it so well! You court the limelight with energy, thrusting yourself into prominence, for the applause of the crowd makes you feel good inside. Sometimes it may seem as if you were born fortunate, but there may come a time when you realise that plaudits are empty, and it truly takes more than the admiration of others to create a mature, self-actualising man or woman. Now begins your greatest adventure – an introspective journey that admits the presence of hurts as well as bliss and that enables you to assess and develop the person within. What is *really* of value to you? When you have discovered this you may truly applaud yourself.

## Aries Sun / Virgo Moon

You are not a person to tangle with in debate, for your logic is relentless and you waste no energy on wondering how your opponent may feel. Treading on corns? Nonsense! It's the facts that matter. You are mega-efficient, and you are your own worst critic. You have a mind like a steel trap – energetic precision is your phrase. The only danger is that you may undermine your wonderful abilities in self-criticism. You need to learn to appreciate yourself in your imperfections, for we all have them. Also you need to get used to taking steps forwards before you have dusted away all the obstacles – have faith that they will disappear as you go. Learning to love yourself with all the faults that make you human will enable you to love others and thus feel warmed and fulfilled.

## Aries Sun / Libra Moon

Often you get really frustrated with yourself. Just as you think your mind is truly made up and you are about to launch yourself into action, you suddenly see the other side, the alternative action or viewpoint. Your need for peaceful surroundings stops you from making changes. Sometimes something holds you back from showing righteous anger. In the end you will find that asserting yourself when necessary is the only true way to inner peace and you can sail to the shores of self-fulfilment only by rocking the boat on the way. You don't lack the courage, but you may lack the belief in yourself. Create beautiful surroundings for yourself and develop your intuition, for you were born when the Moon was full and potentially you have psychic gifts. Also take note of your dreams, for they may be prophetic. They are sure to help you in finding inner harmony if you study them with an open mind.

## Aries Sun / Scorpio Moon

Just when you think it is all perfectly clear and the way is open for action; when you know what's happening and what everyone is going to, then something comes up and bites you on the posterior! You may be ignoring your own intense emotions, but others may be getting mixed messages. Try not to blame them for being devious, nefarious or controlling. Try to ask yourself honestly – for guts are your great gift – where you are passing up your own emotions, because they seem too mucky, preferring to concentrate on the job in hand, ever forwards and upwards. You are a strongly sexual person, but you do have other needs, and these may be very baby-like and distorted from neglect. True self-possession comes from facing and knowing yourself, not from controlling others, who are sure to sense this. If you face yourself and be gentle with your own needs you can become very powerful.

## Aries Sun / Sagittarius Moon

It's people like you who brought humankind out of the caves (which were no doubt originally discovered and painted with surging herds of aurochs and bison by people like you!). No doubt it was an Aries Sun/Sagittarius Moon who discovered fire! You love pushing back frontiers, both intellectual and physical, all with devil-may-care bonhomie. You are an explorer, innovator, adventurer and no walls can hold you. Sometimes you may feel quite god or goddess like – and there's the rub! Occasionally you may be a bit too big for your boots, but that is a way of escaping your vulnerability, and you need to remind yourself that one of the tasks for which you are best suited is to find the true deity within. You will not have such compulsive needs to push back boundaries if you feel the true inner freedom that comes from a spiritual guiding centre. Develop a loving philosophy that tolerates your own and other people's limitations. Seek the truth, but never allow yourself to believe you have found the Ultimate, for only in openness are you truly wise.

## Aries Sun / Capricorn Moon

You can be quite relentless when it comes to achieving goals and you like to be upwardly mobile at a steady, if not meteoric rate. Financial security and material status are important to you, and you put all your energy into achieving these, identifying obstacles and demolishing them systematically. Never let it be said (and I doubt if it ever will be!) that you did not rise to a challenge! Did you ever ask yourself what you are trying to prove, and to whom? And do your acquisitions and triumphs really bring you peace? To achieve true inner security perhaps you need to step back and ask yourself what you really need, what is really worthwhile, and tell yourself it is okay to be vulnerable. Only then, in the strength of self-acceptance, can you feel really powerful and effectual.

## Aries Sun / Aquarius Moon

This may be a zany combination and you may be a dreamer, your mind preoccupied by extra-terrestrials, UFOs or the latest sci-fi movie. There may not seem to be enough of interest in the ordinary world and you may be easily bored. You have a scientific bent, and you may be a highly inventive and original person. What are you really trying to escape from? Your intuition is good, and you need to use it to discover more about your inner needs and who and what you are, rather than fleeing from such considerations. You will be more free, more able to take decisive action, if you are able to be open to your inner self and the needs, wounds and vulnerabilities we all carry. The only truly free person is one who accepts herself or himself, and who has the imagination to appreciate this if not you?

## Aries Sun / Pisces Moon

You may be the most introverted type of Aries and you need space to explore your inner world. You are generous and it is important to you to feel that you are being effective in helping someone and doing your bit for the common good. Or you may feel ashamed of your inner feelings and they may hold you back, like soggy feathers, whenever you try to soar. Like Sir Walter Raleigh, your grand gestures may leave you with a wet cloak. What are the visions that are really important to you? How can you make contact with your source of spirit within? You may have lost sight of your true needs in acting out the desires of others. You may be acting in a self-centred way and yet feeling bad about it, or you may be manipulating others to give you the freedom you need. Meditate and give yourself permission to have what you legitimately want, for only then will you have anything real to give.

# Appendix 2

## ZODIACAL COMPATIBILITY

To assess fully the compatibility of two people an astrologer needs to have the entire chart of each individual, and while Sun-sign factors will be noticeable there is a legion of other important points to be taken into account. Venus and Mercury are always very close to the Sun, and while these are often in the Sun sign, so intensifying its effect, they may also fall in one of the signs lying on either side of your Sun sign. So, as an 'Aries' you may have Venus and/or Mercury in Taurus or Pisces, and this will increase your empathy with these signs. In addition the Moon and all the other planets including the Ascendant and Midheaven need to be taken into account. So if you have always been drawn to Scorpio people, perhaps you have Moon or Ascendant in Scorpio.

In order to give a vivid character sketch things have to be stated graphically. You should look for the dynamics at work, rather than be too literal about interpretation – for instance, you may find that you do not argue much with Scorpios, but you may still be aware of an intensity. It is up to the two of you whether a relationship works, for it can if you are both committed. Part of that is using the awareness you have to help, not necessarily as a reason for abandoning the relationship. There are always points of compatibility, and we are here to learn from each other.

On a scale of 1 (worst) to 4 (best), here is a table to assess instantly the superficial compatibility rating between Aries and companions:

| | |
|---|---|
| Aries 3 | Libra 1 |
| Taurus 2 | Scorpio 1 |
| Gemini 4 | Sagittarius 4 |
| Cancer 1 | Capricorn 2 |
| Leo 4 | Aquarius 2 |
| Virgo 3 | Pisces 3 |

## ■ ARIES COMPATIBILITIES

### Aries with Aries

This is a forceful combination indeed. You are likely to have lots of arguments, but as neither of you takes offence that deeply, usually this will not be too much of a problem. The exception could be when one of the pair truly oversteps the mark and undying enmity ensues. Not that Aries bears a grudge, but icy indifference may take a long time to thaw. Give each other plenty of space and count to ten!

**As lovers**    There is lots of passion in this relationship, and a great deal of drama. Both of you will be high on the emotion and idealism of it all. As with many combinations of Fire signs it may be a case of 'Am I a figment of your imagination, or are you a figment of mine?' Both of you will work at keeping romance alive and the success of this will depend of whether the ideas of romance coincide. Aries woman wants a stimulating intellectual side to the relationship, while Aries man may be bent on proving his sexual prowess again . . . and again . . . and again.

**As friends**    Your friendship is likely to be about doing things together, rather than just 'being'. Disagreements are likely, but at least you won't find each other a drag!

**As business partners** Unless each of you has substantial modifying factors in your individual charts, a business partnership with just two Aries is not a good idea. Both of you want to be the 'ideas' person, both want to run the show, and neither are that brilliant at controlling financial outflow. This can work best if each of you has a separate role, where you can be unilaterally dynamic, and get in a Capricorn or Taurus to advise on the business angle.

## Aries with Taurus

This is a bit like the irresistible force meeting the immovable object! Surprisingly, it can work, because the two of you seem to inhabit parallel universes, and may be able to ignore the differences – most of the time, at least! Together you can be very creative. Aries will need to work hard at being as patient as possible and to realise that Taurus does see things very differently, but that such perceptions are also valid and useful. Aries can open up Taurean horizons and find much to enjoy in the process.

**As lovers** Ms Taurus can really fascinate Mr Aries as she's so sensual and identified with her body, while Ms Aries finds Mr Taurus so strong, silent and sexy. Trouble can set in if Aries feels restricted or Taurus insecure, so you will both need to be aware of this. Both of you are stubborn in different ways, but as long as Taurus' comfort isn't threatened and Aries is given the time to calm down after disagreements (which often doesn't take long) you should be able to weather the storm. Sex is important to you both, for different reasons, and you should make every effort to keep excitement alive.

**As friends** You have a lot to show each other as you have quite different perceptions of life. Aries can enliven Taurus, while Taurus can show Aries delights he or she had never formerly hung around long enough to notice.

**As business partners** This can work very well indeed providing each has her or his own niche, Aries has room to pursue his or her brilliant ideas and Taurus holds the purse strings. Taurus may get worried about the risks Aries takes, but will become mollified when some of the risks pay off handsomely. Aries often has a nose for a business opportunity while Taurus has the sense to keep it all within bounds.

## Aries with Gemini

These two get on very well, for Aries finds Gemini endlessly fascinating and enjoys the unpredictability and liveliness of the sign. Gemini finds Aries stimulating (most people do!) and will keep returning to have more and more ideas and impressions sparked off by this fiery soul. The drawback may be that Aries becomes a little too intense for Gemini at times, while Aries may find Gemini a bit hard to pin down and enlist when he or she is on a crusade.

**As lovers** Ms Aries enjoys a man who can really talk to her and loves the way he articulates his feelings. However, she may find him a little cool in intimate moments. Mr Aries finds lively Gemini a turn-on. Hopefully he won't notice that her heart isn't necessarily behind his chosen cause, because her eyes are so clear and intent, and she not only hangs on his every word but has just the right thing of her own to say. These two may have trouble staying faithful, but sometimes neither may mind too much, and if the love is strong they will always find their way back.

**As friends** An excellent combination for fun and excitement. There may be plenty of laughter and chatter. Aries will think of things to do and Gemini will suggest clever refinements and add 'style' – or Gemini will have the suggestions and Aries will put them into action.

**As business partners**   There is a lot to be said for the two of you in business together, for you each have the mental speed to seize opportunities. Gemini is better at thinking things through than Aries and may perceive snags. However, he or she is less likely to obstruct than to suggest appropriate modifications. Occasionally Gemini may become nervous of Aries' taste for taking risks, and will need to invent suitable strategies for protection.

## Aries with Cancer

This is a difficult combination. All the Water signs are sensitive, but Cancer is perhaps the most touchy and the most readily hurt and offended by Arien brashness. A lot of work is needed on both sides to make this twosome succeed. Cancer does have bags of imagination, and will need to draw on all of it to understand Aries. Aries really needs to negotiate plenty of space for her or himself at the start of any association, for subsequent attempts to gain it may get shipwrecked.

**As lovers**   There may be a lot of deep feeling and arousal at first, and Aries will be drawn to the Cancerian depth. However, the clinginess of Cancer may become unbearable for Aries and the Cancerian caution may be seen as 'your eternal negativity'. Ms Cancer does admire Mr Aries' ability to be decisive and she may intrigue him at first. Ms Aries feels sure that all Mr Cancer needs is a dynamic woman in his life and he will succeed, while he may be inspired by her. Trouble can set in later when each gets disappointed and the sex life may be the first casualty as repressed resentments smoulder at bedtime. Cancer is one sign that may make Aries 'give up'. Don't. Work it through.

**As friends**   You are most likely to be drawn together because you share some belief. Aries may galvanise Cancer into some sort of action and if Cancer is very patient he or she may just teach Aries a little bit of tact.

**As business partners**   Again Cancer is likely to frustrate Aries and throw a wet blanket on the flames of enthusiasm. Cancer just doesn't like risks at all, while Aries lives by them. This is another combination that works best if each has his or her own sphere, although Cancer will get very worried if he or she doesn't know what Aries is doing – especially with the money. Handling of personnel, clients and any sensitive matter is best passed to Cancer.

## Aries with Leo

These two are in perpetual competition and each will no doubt accuse the other of being self-centred and bossy. However, as neither of them take this particularly as an insult there is every possibility that this stormy relationship could continue. There is so much warmth and bonhomie to share and much love may be generated and expressed.

**As lovers**   This is an extremely passionate combination. Each is idealistic and romantic and sex between the two may be an ever-burning flame. Ms Leo is enraptured to know that she has finally met a man who knows how a queen should be treated, and he is only too pleased to play Sir Lancelot. Mr Leo is delighted to have such a vibrant female with him, to do him credit at all times and occasions. This couple may be very generous with each other in terms of time, money and affection, but there are sure to be some explosive rows!

**As friends**   The two Fire signs have much in common and should find plenty to enthuse over together. They can inspire each other to greater heights and find each other interesting in every way. Some form of competition is likely between the two, which may be ongoing, for although both signs enjoy competition neither likes to admit defeat.

**As business partners**   In this arena each has considerable respect for the other. Leo delights in the Arien entrepreneurial skills while Aries loves Leo's grand and sweeping approach. Leo does love to take the limelight and trouble could ensue when Leo claims, by inference, that all the triumphs are her or his own. Leo just might not appreciate Aries enough at all times, and Aries may be a little too autonomous for controlling Leo. Their main problem is likely to be money, for both are extravagant. A Taurus would make a good third partner.

## Aries with Virgo

Strangely, there is a very pernickety side to Aries and Virgo may come as a delight. Virgo can find many, many things to complain about and Aries will happily do the complaining – loudly and at great length. The fascination of Fire for Earth reappears here, and there may be a strong attraction. Of course, there are also many contrasts and work will be needed to overcome them. Aries takes a bird's eye view and Virgo an ant's eye view, and so it may seem as if they are looking at a different universe.

**As lovers**   Sex is a powerful force between these two. The self-possessedness of Virgo is irresistible to the Ram, and he or she will do anything to conquer that reserve and expose the secret core of sensuality. Virgo finds the passion of Aries is like a burst of sunshine and she or he may warm to it – in good time, of course. Ms Aries finds Mr Virgo suave and super-cool, while he is devastated by this woman's verve and charm. Mr Aries finds Ms Virgo compellingly sexy – the original 'long, cool woman in a black dress', and will stop at nothing to win her, while she looks on enigmatically (but with growing approval). This partnership can be an enduring one if Virgo will try not to limit Aries, and if Aries will try to tolerate being tidied-up after.

**As friends**  Virgo can certainly show Aries how to organise her or his life better, and Aries may just tolerate this as it makes things run so much more smoothly. Virgo will be good at organising all the Ram's bright ideas and they should be able to enjoy themselves together, although they are sure to get irritable with each other quite regularly.

**As business partners**  A good combination, where Virgo dots the 'i's' and crosses the 't's' on the contracts. Because Virgo is so efficient he or she is less likely to become nervous at Arien extravaganza, knowing quite well how to keep it all in order. This can only go so far, however, and no one worries like a Virgo at anything that seems to be going over the top. Aries needs to be very communicative in this case.

## Aries with Libra

These signs are opposite each other on the zodiac wheel. Thus they both complement each other and can be a continual thorn in the other's side. Aries can find Libra's air of detached urbanity and smooth evasiveness quite infuriating, while Libra finds Aries insufferable. Aries may be rude to Libra, while Libra strenuously resents decisions being made for him or her (even if he or she refuses to make them for him or herself). However, these two have much to offer each other if they will look honestly at the relationship and within themselves. Libra can see that Aries irritates because he or she possesses the decisiveness that Libra lacks, while Aries can perceive that tact and diplomacy really do work at times.

**As lovers**  Librans usually manage to create an ambience of beauty, and Aries can find this seductive. Libra may find Aries crude, but sometimes 'a bit of rough' can be a turn-on – and anyway, Libra reasons that Aries can be refined. Strangely, this may actually prove true if the sensual rewards are great enough. These signs share a taste for style, making lots of potential pizzazz.

**As friends** These will argue constantly, with Aries attacking and Libra parrying. Libra is likely to take up a position of moral superiority as the peacemaker, while Aries gets more and more frustrated at somehow being rendered ineffectual. However, they may share ideological interests.

**As business partners** This can work best of all, for Aries has the ideas while Libra has the gift of dealing with people and 'knowing a man who can'. Trouble may arise when the time comes to sign on the dotted line. At this point Libra hesitates while Aries, pen in hand, is straining to get the boring bit over. Also while Aries spends thoughtlessly, Libra also spends – thoughtfully. Consider an Earth sign third partner.

## Aries with Scorpio

Feelings run high between these two signs and they may decide to give each other a wide berth. Conversely, they may be irresistibly drawn together by a fatal fascination. Aries is ruled by Mars, and before the discovery of Pluto, Scorpio too was believed to be ruled by the fiery planet, and Scorpio was called 'the night house of Mars'. Both of these signs can fight, and they may remain locked in conflict. Scorpio is much more subtle and Aries may be deeply wounded, concealing wounds in anger.

**As lovers** Needless to say, passion can run very high with these two and sexuality is likely to be steamy. Aries will not understand Scorpio's manipulation of sex to gain his or her own ends and may end up frustrated. A lot of work is needed if this partnership is to work, and a great deal of honesty. Such a relationship can take you both to the heights and appear karmic in intensity, or it can leave two lives in tatters. Both of you are proud and uncompromising. Learn to appreciate that in each other.

**As friends** You may not be drawn together as friends, for friendship may be too milky a solution for natures of such extremes. However, if you do become friends it is likely that you would almost die for each other, sharing confidences and experiences given to no other. Be careful neither of you betray this.

**As business partners** Problems will arise due to Scorpio's need to know everything and control everything – and his or her inevitable success in doing so. Aries may feel he or she has no freedom and may become more and more unpredictable, while Scorpio becomes more invasive and more subtle by the day. However, you both have tremendous drive and are resourceful in complementary ways. Honesty again is vital, and not least with oneself!

## Aries with Sagittarius

Another Fire-sign combination, full of belly-laughs and adventure. Sagittarius loves the exuberance of Aries and in Sagittarius Aries finds the perfect match – mentor, encourager and comrade-in-arms. As with all mixtures of two Fire signs the problem is that reality, in the day-to-day sense, gets left far behind in the quest for meanings and excitement.

**As lovers** A very warm and highly sexual partnership. Both of you may enjoy sexual experimentation and neither of you is all that prone to remaining faithful. However, as neither of you is generally sensitive, an 'open marriage' or similar relationship may appeal. Care needs to be taken here, for Sagittarius's propensity for interpreting the rules according to his or her own advantage may send Aries into a storm of anger – Sagittarius is a sign that can make even Aries insecure! Ms Sagittarius loves the way Aries can stimulate her, satisfy her and yet respect her individuality, and Mr Aries relishes being with such an undemanding female. This is fine, until the wishes and needs of one conflict with those of the other – after all, who is going to hold the baby if you are both going out, and have both forgotten to arrange a babysitter?

**As friends** These two make good mates, and will enjoy doing many things together, competing intellectually or sportingly and generally heightening each other's appreciation of life.

**As business partners** A really lively combination, this is a make-or-break formula. Sagittarius is tireless when it comes to thinking up new ideas, following leads and using the imagination. To Sagittarius the 'sky's the limit' and Aries can get really carried away. It may be Aries who gets worried that expansion is going out of control and may feel Sagittarius is somewhat wild. A more practical third partner should be involved.

## Aries with Capricorn

Both of you are very ambitious and both of you are convinced that you know the best way to do anything and everything – as these ways are generally totally different, some conflict is inevitable. However, as each observes that the other does get results, mutual respect may develop.

**As lovers** Earth and Fire are often strongly attracted, and Aries and Capricorn are likely to be deeply smitten with each other. Aries finds the sophistication of Capricorn very magnetic, while Capricorn finds Arien exuberance endearing, as long as Aries isn't too impractical. The sexual side of this relationship will be exciting and enduring, in all probability. Ms Capricorn adores Mr Aries' physicality, although she won't be over quick to respond, which will serve to increase Arien ardour. Ms Aries finds Mr Capricorn very supportive of all her schemes. The danger in this relationship is that Aries may get bored if Capricorn is too slow, although Capricorn's restraint, without coyness is irresistible to the Ram.

**As friends**   You have much to offer each other, for Aries has all the enthusiasm in the world, and Capricorn has all the method. Thus the Ram will feel deeply gratified as Capricorn puts all the treasured plans into practice. Occasionally Aries may accuse Capricorn of being obstructive, but after a while, as Capricorn is inevitably proved right, Aries relents.

**As business partners**   These two are excellent in business together, although Capricorn had better be boss. Capricorn is inexhaustibly practical and will continually seek to use all Aries' ideas, modifying them where necessary to make them viable. Capricorn is usually good with money, and should hold the purse strings.

## Aries with Aquarius

These two form an unusual combination which is likely to be whacky and unpredictable. Aquarius is far too detached for Aries to feel comfortable, and the Aquarian habit of saying what he or she thinks instead of what he or she is going to do – or even telling Aries what Aries thinks! – can send the Ram, into orbit. Nonetheless, the independence of Aquarius will usually earn the Arien respect.

**As lovers**   The Ram is likely to find Aquarius rather aloof and dispassionate and may become very frustrated. Both signs like to be friends as well as lovers, but Aries may not understand that Aquarius is often comfortable with little more than friendship. Ms Aries loves being with a man who respects her independence, but she may become very bitchy when he doesn't seem to appreciate how sexy she is – which will just cause Mr Aquarius to withdraw to a position of detachment and even less responsiveness. Mr Aries is drawn to this striking Aquarian lady, but may not understand her need to keep him at arm's length so much of the time. To make this relationship work, Aquarius may need to risk greater intimacy. Each may enjoy a fling outside the relationship.

**As friends**  You may argue a lot, but Aquarius handles the Ram's impetuousness by ignoring it much of the time, while Aries admires the unconventional attitudes of Aquarius. Possibly you will share a zany and irreverent humour, and find each other stimulating.

**As business partners**  Aries will never be afraid to put an unusual idea into practice if it looks viable, and Aquarius is often full of new and unorthodox ways of doing things. Aries may get annoyed at Aquarius' apparent inability to get fired up about anything, and the Aquarian habit of retreating to the stratosphere when problems or conflicts arise could mean some things never get sorted. Capricorn influence can help.

## Aries with Pisces

Strange as it may seem, a combination of the unstoppable Ram with the sensitive Fish often goes very well, especially at the start. Pisces is indulgent of Aries' exuberance and tolerates his or her brashness, while Aries adores the Piscean responsiveness. Pisces will usually let the Ram have his or her own way on the surface and quietly get on with what he or she deems necessary.

**As lovers**  This can be sensational. Pisces basks in the passion of this fiery sign, who never lets Aries forget how desirable and wonderful he or she is, while Aries is spurred to ever greater heights by such appreciation. Ms Aries rejoices that she has found a man who can understand her and treat her so sensitively, while Ms Pisces is thrilled to bits with her dashing Galahad. Trouble can set in if Aries becomes too insensitive and impatient and Pisces begins to complain. Pisces cannot respond sexually in a climate of disonnance and this may make the Ram wild and full of accusations of manipulation (which may be well-founded). If Aries can remember to buy a special present to say sorry, and if Pisces can assemble all her or his native wisdom, this partnership can work.

**As friends** Pisces may find that he or she is constantly helping Aries to achieve desires and that the friendship is all one way. For this to work, Pisces needs to identify her or his needs and ensure that Aries knows about them.

**As business partners** Both these signs are highly intuitive in their different ways and may find they are able to make a lot of money. Aries can smell out a good proposition at a hundred paces while Pisces always 'knows' who to trust. However, as with so many Aries partnerships, money could be a real problem unless a practical third party comes in.

# Appendix 3

## ■ TRADITIONAL ASSOCIATIONS AND TOTEM

Each sign of the zodiac is said to have an affinity with certain colours, plants, stones and other substances. Of course, we cannot be definite about this, for not only do sources vary regarding specific correspondences – we also have the rest of the astrological chart to bear in mind. Some people also believe that the whole concept of such associations is invalid. However, there certainly do seem to be some links between the character of each of the signs and the properties of certain substances. It is up to you to experiment, and to see what works for you.

Anything that traditionally links with Aries is liable to intensify Arien traits. So if you wish for some reason to remain calm and passive, you should steer clear of the colour red, and broom or carnations! However, if you want to be your Arien, enterprising best, it may help to surround yourself with the right stimuli, especially on a down day. Here are some suggestions:

- **Colours**  Shades of red – possibly all bright colours and strong contrasts.
- **Flowers**  Broom, carnation, nettle, dandelion.
- **Metal**  Iron and steel.
- **Stones**  Bloodstone, garnet, ruby.

## Aromatherapy

Aromatherapy uses the healing power of essential oils both to prevent ill health and to maintain good health. Specific oils can sometimes be used to treat specific ailments. Essential oils are concentrated and powerful substances and should be treated with respect. Buy from a reputable source. *Do not use any oil in pregnancy* until you have checked it is OK with a reputable source (see Further Reading). *Do not ingest oils* – they act through the subtle medium of smell, and are absorbed in massage. *Do not place undiluted in the skin.* For massage: Dilute in a carrier oil such as sweet almond or grapeseed, two drops of oil to one teaspoon of carrier. Use in an oil burner, six to ten drops at each time, to fragrance your living area.

### Essential oils

- **Basil**  A nerve tonic, will help if you are over-wrought and good for respiratory infections.
- **Cedarwood**  Good to stabilise the mind, for grounding and a general tonic. Also relieves nervous tension.
- **Cinnamon**  Warming and stimulating, good for combatting fatigue. Antifungal. May irritate the skin, so use low concentration.
- **Peppermint**  Great for the heartburn that Aries sometimes get, for clearing the head and for anxiety. This makes a wonderful footbath if a few drops are added to a bowl of water.
- **Pine**  Used for facial steaming, this oil cleanses the pores. Generally invigorating and good for all types of colds and 'flu. Good as a room deodoriser, especially when it is hot.

Naturally you are not restricted to oils ruled by your sign, for in many cases treatment by other oils will be beneficial. You should consult a qualified aromatherapist for advice if you have a particular problem. If any health problem persists, see your GP.

## Your birth totem

According to the tradition of certain native North American tribes, each of the signs of the zodiac is known by a totem animal. The idea of the totem animal is useful, for animals are powerful, living symbols and they can do much to put us in touch with our own potentials. Knowing your totem animal is different from knowing your sign, for your sign is used to define and describe you – as we have been doing in this book – whereas your totem shows you a path of potential learning and growth.

The totem for Aries is the Falcon, and you also have affinity with Eagle and Hawk. You were born in the Awakening Time. There is a difficulty here, for the North American lore is based on the seasonal cycle. Thus for those of you living in the Southern Hemisphere, it may be worth bearing in mind the totems of your opposite sign, Libra. These are Crow, also Grizzly Bear and possibly Butterfly, although this relates to the Air Element and the Libran time is called Falling Leaves Time.

The falcon is a bird of prey. It trusts to its own strength, to the wind and to the elements. The eyes of the falcon are sharp, eternally scanning the landscape for all that moves. In this way Falcon people are alert for every sensation, every stimulus and new idea. Seeing something worthwhile, they may swoop without hesitation, and as the falcon takes its prey back into the skies, so Falcon people take with them what can enhance life. Falcons can see the broad panorama. Theirs is the realm of the spirit, of the sunburst of dawn over the land. These birds lay their eggs on ledges, trusting to wind and sky, and while they are beautiful they are not cuddly creatures. As a symbol, Falcon is a link to possibilities of all kinds, to courage, enterprise, imagination, vision and freedom. Falcon is a totem with which to travel far and fast, on the rush of the wind. The liberty, power, scope and speed of this bird can link you to your own similar qualities.

## Contacting your totem

You can use visualisation techniques to make contact with the energies of your birth totem. You will need to be very quiet, still and relaxed. Make sure you won't be disturbed. Have a picture of your totem before you, and perhaps burn one of the oils we have mentioned, in an oil burner, to intensify the atmosphere. When you are ready, close your eyes, and imagine that you are your totem animal – imagine how it feels, what it sees, smells, hears. What are its feelings, instincts and abilities. Keep this up for as long as you are comfortable, then come back to everyday awareness. Write down your experiences, and eat or drink something, to ground you. This can be a wonderfully refreshing and mind-clearing exercise, and you may find it inspiring. Naturally, if you feel you have other totem animals – creatures with which you feel an affinity – you are welcome to visualise those. Look out for your totems in the wild – there may be a message for you.

# Further reading
## and resources

*Astrology for Lovers*, Liz Greene, Unwin, 1986. The title may be misleading, for this is a serious, yet entertaining and wickedly accurate account of the signs. A table is included to help you find your Rising Sign. This book is highly recommended.

*Teach Yourself Astrology*, Jeff Mayo and Christine Ramsdale, Hodder & Stoughton, 1996. A classic textbook for both beginner and practising astrologer, giving a fresh insight to birth charts through a unique system of personality interpretation.

*Love Signs for Beginners*, Kristyna Arcarti, Hodder & Stoughton, 1995. A practical introduction to the astrology of romantic relationships, explaining the different roles played by each of the planets and focussing particularly on the position of the Moon at the time of birth.

*Star Signs for Beginners*, Kristyna Arcarti, Hodder & Stoughton, 1993. An analysis of each of the star signs – a handy, quick reference.

*The Moon and You for Beginners*, Teresa Moorey, Hodder & Stoughton, 1996. Discover how the phase of the Moon when you were born affects your personality. This book looks at the nine lunar types – how they live, love, work and play, and provides simple tables to enable you to find out your birth phase and which type you are.

*The New Compleat Astrologer*, Derek and Julia Parker, Mitchell Beazley, 1984. This is a complete introduction to astrology with instructions on chart calculation and planetary tables, as well as clear and interesting descriptions of planets and signs. Including history and reviewing present-day astrology, this is an extensive work, in glossy, hardback form, with colour illustrations.

*The Knot of Time: Astrology and the Female Experience*, Lindsay River and Sally Gillespie. For personal growth, from a gently feminine perspective, this book has much wisdom.

*The Astrology of Self-discovery*, Tracy Marks, CRCS Publications, 1985. This book is especially useful for Moon signs.

*The Astrologer's Handbook*, Francis Sakoian and Louis Acker, Penguin, 1984. This book explains chart calculation and takes the reader through the meanings of signs and planets, with extensive interpretations of planets in signs and houses. In addition, all the major aspects between planets and angles are interpreted individually. A very useful work.

*Aromatherapy for Pregnancy and Childbirth*, Margaret Fawcett RGN, RM, LLSA, Element, 1993.

*The Aromatherapy Handbook*, Daniel Ryman, C W Daniel, 1990.

## Useful addresses

### The Faculty of Astrological Studies

The claim of the Faculty to provide the 'finest and most comprehensive astrological tuition in the world' is well founded. Correspondence courses of a high calibre are offered, leading to the internationally recognised diploma. Evening classes, seminars and summer schools are taught, catering for the complete beginner to the most experienced astrologer. A list of trained consultants can be supplied on request, if you wish for a chart interpretation. For further details telephone (UK code) 0171 700 3556 (24-hour answering service); or fax 0171 700 6479. Alternatively, you can write, with SAE, to: Ref. T. Moorey, FAS., BM7470, London WC1N 3XX, UK.

**Educational**

California Institute of Integral Studies, 765 Ashbury St, San Francisco, CA 94117. Tel: (415) 753-6100

Kepler College of Astrological Arts and Sciences, 4518 University Way, NE, Suite 213, Seattle, WA 98105. Tel: (206) 633-4907

Robin Armstrong School of Astrology, Box 5265, Station 'A', Toronto, Ontario, M5W 1N5, Canada. Tel: (416) 923-7827

Vancouver Astrology School, Astraea Astrology, Suite 412, 2150 W Broadway, Vancouver, V6K 4L9, Canada. Tel: (604) 536-3880

The Southern Cross Academy of Astrology, PO Box 781147, Sandton, SA 2146 (South Africa) Tel: 11-468-1157; Fax: 11-468-1522

**Periodicals**

*American Astrology Magazine*, PO Box 140713, Staten Island, NY 10314-0713. e-mail: am.astrology@genie.gies,com

*The Journal of the Seasons*, PO Box 5266, Wellesley St, Auckland 1, New Zealand. Tel/fax: (0)9-410-8416

*The Federation of Australian Astrologers Bulletin*, PO Box 159, Stepney, SA 5069. Tel/fax: 8-331-3057

*Aspects*, PO Box 2968, Rivonia, SA 2128 (South Africa) Tel: 11-864-1436

*Realta*, The Journal of the Irish Astrological Association, 4 Quay Street, Galway, Ireland. Available from IAA, 193, Lwr Rathmines Rd, Dublin 6, Ireland.

*Astrological Association*, 396 Caledonian Road, London, N1 1DN. Tel: (UK code) 0171 700 3746; Fax: 0171 700 6479. Bi-monthly journal issued.